D0479799

Response to
Intervention

I dedicate my work for this book to my boys,
Scott and Wesley. It is your love, patience, and encouragement
that have made this possible. You are the joy of my life, and I can never
thank you enough for all that you are and all that you do.

—*Cara Shores*

I'd like to dedicate my work for this book to
my wife, Dr. Renet L. Bender, who has assisted me in a
variety of ways over the years. Her help and support make many things
possible, and I thank her for that support and her understanding love.
My life is infinitely richer with her in it.

—*William N. Bender*

Response to Intervention

Intervention

— A Practical Guide for Every Teacher —

William N. Bender
Cara Shores

A Joint Publication

Council for
Exceptional
Children

CORWIN PRESS
A SAGE Publications Company
Thousand Oaks, CA 91320

Copyright © 2007 by Corwin Press, Inc.

All rights reserved. When forms and sample documents are included, their use is authorized only by educators, local school sites, and/or noncommercial or nonprofit entities who have purchased the book. Except for that usage, no part of this book may be reproduced or utilized in any form or by any means, electronic or mechanical, including photocopying, recording, or by any information storage and retrieval system, without permission in writing from the publisher.

For information:

Corwin Press
A Sage Publications Company
2455 Teller Road
Thousand Oaks, California 91320
www.corwinpress.com

Sage Publications Ltd.
1 Oliver's Yard
55 City Road
London EC1Y 1SP
United Kingdom

Sage Publications India Pvt Ltd
B 1/I 1 Mohan Cooperative
   Industrial Area
Mathura Road, New Delhi 110 044
India

Sage Publications Asia-Pacific Pte Ltd
33 Pekin Street #02-01
Far East Square
Singapore 048763

Printed in the United States of America

Library of Congress Cataloging-in-Publication Data

Bender, William N.
Response to intervention : a practical guide for every teacher /
William N. Bender, Cara Shores.
      p. cm.
Includes bibliographical references and index.
ISBN 978-1-4129-5385-6 (cloth : alk. paper)
ISBN 978-1-4129-5386-3 (pbk. : alk. paper)
   1. Remedial teaching. 2. Learning disabled children—Education.
3. Learning disabilities—Diagnosis. I. Shores, Cara. II. Title.

LB1029.R4B46 2007
371.9—dc22

2006102698

This book is printed on acid-free paper.

07   08   09   10   11   10   9   8   7   6   5   4   3   2

Acquisitions Editor:	Allyson P. Sharp
Editorial Assistant:	Nadia Kashper
Production Editor:	Catherine M. Chilton
Copy Editor:	Annette R. Pagliaro Sweeney
Typesetter:	C&M Digitals (P) Ltd.
Proofreader:	Doris Hus
Indexer:	Marilyn Augst, Prairie Moon Indexing
Cover Designer:	Monique Hahn
Graphic Designer:	Lisa Miller

Contents

Preface

An Open Letter to Educators

Within the next two or three years, education will change rather dramatically, because of the implementation of Response to Intervention (RTI) procedures across the nation. Teachers in both general and special education classes will find their jobs transformed as we move into a research-proven instructional method that will benefit many children who are challenged by the academic content. In fact, all students will benefit from implementation of this procedure, as teachers become more fluent in truly individualized progress monitoring and instruction.

While this change is prompted by several legislative measures including the No Child Left Behind (NCLB) legislation, and more specifically, the 2004 Reauthorization of Individuals with Disabilities Education Act (IDEA), this metamorphosis is much broader than merely a new way to document the existence of a learning disability. All educators will become involved in implementation of programs to demonstrate how students respond on an individual basis to various educational interventions. Most of the early work required by the RTI procedures for a particular child will take place in the general education classroom. Thus, this initiative will not only affect special educators; all educators will be expected to implement this procedure in their classes. This book is intended as a practical guide to assist those teachers in what, for many, will be a new and untried instructional procedure.

We strongly support this renewed emphasis on monitoring students' response to educational interventions. In fact, frequent progress monitoring and implementation of specific educational interventions based on that monitoring—the essence of RTI—has been proven to be among the best instructional practices available. Although this book is not intended as an exhaustive review of research on RTI, we do discuss the most influential studies as a backdrop for understanding RTI.

Moreover, because teachers across the nation will be challenged to understand and implement these procedures in their classrooms, this book provides specific examples of how to implement RTI. Both general educators and special educators will be required to apply research-proven educational interventions; monitor student progress daily or weekly; and plan additional, more intensive educational interventions for students who are not progressing adequately. Thus, RTI is likely to affect almost every classroom in the nation; virtually every student will see their teachers become more sensitive to individualized academic progress.

In short, this is not merely another initiative; this move to RTI promises to reform education in very significant ways, as educators in every classroom instruct and monitor progress on an individual basis for many of their students. Clearly, this is not business as usual. Within two years, it will become the responsibility of almost every teacher in the nation to develop skills for RTI and implement RTI in their classes.

With that in mind, we believe this book can be of great use for educators nationwide. We have made every effort to present rigorous examples of RTI procedures, and also to indicate where and how educators may save time while taking on these new and challenging responsibilities. We have provided many opportunities for reflection on the RTI procedures discussed throughout the chapters, and all educators are encouraged to use those reflections within the chapters to consider how RTI might be implemented in their own class. Finally, although RTI has received recent interest as one way to document eligibility for students suspected of having a learning disability, there are many other applications of RTI including using the RTI process to curb inappropriate behavior. An example of behaviorally focused RTI is presented here.

As we all move into this new emphasis, we should focus on the benefits of RTI for all children in our classes. RTI is, in effect, one of the best instructional practices we can implement for our students. Implementation of RTI will enhance learning across the board in our classes, and ultimately benefit all of the students whom we serve.

William N. Bender
Cara Shores

Acknowledgments

Corwin Press would like to thank the following reviewers:

Joseph R. Boyle
Associate Professor
Virginia Commonwealth University
Richmond, VA

Jennifer Doolittle
Oregon Department of Education
Salem, OR

Carol H. McClain
Special Populations Management Team
Nebraska Department of Education
Lincoln, NE

Margaret J. McLaughlin
Professor
University of Maryland
College Park, MD

Carla J. Osberg
Program Specialist, Special Populations Office
Nebraska Department of Education
Lincoln, NE

About the Authors

 **William N. Bender**, PhD, taught special education in a junior high school for several years prior to receiving his PhD from the University of North Carolina. He has since published fourteen books and over fifty research articles, and travels widely around the country and Canada doing workshops on differentiated instruction, instructional methodologies, Response to Intervention, ADHD, and disciplinary tactics for special needs students. His use of humor and emphasis on practical strategies for the general and special education classroom make him a favorite among workshop providers; he is often asked to return to the same school for additional workshops on a variety of topics. He currently serves as Professor of Special Education at the University of Georgia.

 **Cara Shores**, EdS, began her career as a special education teacher, and more recently became a co-teacher in an inclusive classroom. She received her master's degree and educational specialist's degree from the University of West Georgia and has since served as Student Support Services Coordinator and District Director of Special Education. Ms. Shores has trained thousands of teachers and administrators across the United States on practical strategies for inclusion, co-teaching, and increasing achievement for all students. She has served as a consultant on several federally funded projects for inclusion and is the principal author of the Georgia Student Support Team Manual. Ms. Shores now serves as the President of Wesley Educational Services.

ABOUT THE CONTRIBUTORS

Victor Morgan, EdS, has spent thirty years in public education dedicated to ensuring that "all" boys and girls receive a quality education. He has served as both a teacher and an administrator, as well as the Director of Student Support Services. He holds an Education Specialist Degree from Jacksonville State University. He has served on a variety of state committees, including the Governor's Office of Educational Accountability Standards Sub-Committee, the Governor's Office of Student Achievement Rewards and Consequences Sub-Committee, The Governor's Education Finance Task Force, and The Governor's Council on Developmental Disabilities Special Education Funding Study Committee. He was recently honored by his peers by receiving the 2004 Lillie Moncus Outstanding Special Education Administrator of the Year Award for Georgia.

Michael R. Baskette, MEd, received his master's degree from Piedmont College, with an emphasis on emotional and behavioral disorders. He has taught for five years in the general education secondary curriculum, and for three years in special education. His research interests include positive behavioral supports, learning disabilities, emotional disturbance, and eligibility procedures. He is currently completing his PhD degree at the University of Georgia.

Lisa Ulmer, MEd, holds a master's degree in special education from Florida State University and is completing her PhD degree at the University of Georgia. She has taught special education for many years in various school districts, and is currently teaching special education at Oconee County High School in Watkinsville, Georgia. Her research interests include learning disabilities eligibility procedures and instructional methods for students with mild disabilities.

1 Response to Intervention

Cara Shores and William N. Bender

With the passage of the Individuals with Disabilities Education Improvement Act (IDEA), the federal government officially allowed students to be classified as learning disabled based on documentation of how well they respond to interventions—a procedure commonly referred to as RTI (Bradley, Danielson, & Doolittle, 2005; Fuchs & Fuchs, 2005; Gersten & Dimino, 2006; Marston, 2005; Mastropieri & Scruggs, 2005; Scruggs & Mastropieri, 2002). IDEA 2004 specifies that, for the purpose of determining learning disability (LD) eligibility, a school district may implement a procedure that involves documentation of how a child responds to scientific, research-based interventions as part of its evaluation procedures.

Although the earliest research on the RTI process began in the 1960s, it has only been in the past decade or so that the process has gained significant momentum among researchers and practitioners as a plausible means of identifying learning and/or reading disabilities. Even so, the process in general terms has been untested for use in determining eligibility, or deciding how students are identified for learning disability services. With that stated, ample evidence exists for use of RTI as a progress-monitoring tool for students with or without disabilities (Fuchs & Fuchs, 2005, 2006; Marston, Muyskens, Lau, & Canter, 2003; Vaughn, Linan-Thompson, & Hickman, 2003; Vellutino et al., 1996).

VALID IDENTIFICATION OF LEARNING DISABILITIES

The exploration of RTI as an approach to LD eligibility determination resulted from the general dissatisfaction with the previous approaches for documentation of a learning disability. In particular, many in the field have expressed dissatisfaction with the discrepancy procedure that documents a disability by demonstrating a large difference between a child's cognitive level (using IQ scores) and his or her achievement. Since the late 1990s, many policymakers have indicated that the discrepancy procedure results in over-identification of students with learning disabilities, and thus, that the procedure seemed to be somewhat inexact in documenting exactly who manifested a learning disability and who did not.

Reflection 1.1	Your Experience With Discrepancies

As an educator, you may have had experiences in documenting a discrepancy for a child suspected of having a learning disability that was less than positive. Have you ever experienced a situation where you were sure, based on reversal errors (e.g., a child reverses letters or words), oral reading errors, or spelling problems, that a child exhibited a learning disability, but the discrepancy was not quite "large enough" to have that student qualified as disabled? What other difficulties have you experienced with implementation of the discrepancy criteria?

The construct for LD was controversial when first included in the Federal Education of the Handicapped Act in 1975, and the controversy continued through the passage of the Individuals with Disabilities Education Act of 1997. Much of the debate stemmed from the use of discrepancies between IQ and achievement as the definitive factor in the definition of Specific Learning Disability (Reschly, Hosp, & Schmied, 2003).

Prior to IDEA of 2004, Specific Learning Disability was defined as:

A disorder in one of more of the basic psychological process involved in understanding or in using language, spoken or written, that may manifest itself in an imperfect ability to listen, think, speak, read, write, spell, or to do mathematical calculations, including conditions such as perceptual disabilities, brain injury, minimal brain dysfunction, dyslexia, and developmental aphasia.

The term does not include learning problems that are primarily the result of visual, hearing, or motor disabilities, of mental retardation, of emotional disturbance, or of environmental, cultural, or economic disadvantage. (U.S. Office of Education, 1977)

In short, the seven areas of Specific Learning Disabilities are listening, thinking, speaking, reading, writing, spelling, and doing mathematical calculations. In addition to delineating these aspects of a learning disability, the law also outlined classification criteria, or rules, which would be used to determine LD eligibility. These criteria did not include low achievement and severe discrepancy, but the criteria did mention basic psychological processes, which is the foundation of Specific Learning Disability. Thus, this definition placed the major emphasis on the severe discrepancy between IQ and achievement, but neither criterion was specifically stated in the definition. In a report submitted to the U.S. Department of Education, Office of Special Education Programs, Reschly, Hosp, and Schmied (2003) identified this inconsistency as a major flaw in the LD construct. They noted that "as definitions and classification criteria have less consistency, increasing problems emerge about meaning and eligibility" (p. 3).

Research has revealed that the severe discrepancy formula as a definition for LD has poor reliability and validity when predicting student achievement (Fletcher, Denton, & Francis, 2005; Siegel, 1989; Vellutino, Scanlon, Small, & Fanuele, 2006; Ysseldyke, 2005). The model is often called a "wait to fail" approach because it is difficult to apply until students are in third grade or beyond (Reschly et al., 2003), because students must be exposed to some level of curricular content in order to have a valid measure of their achievement and calculate a discrepancy between IQ and achievement. Further, over-identification of students with learning disability has increased the overall costs of special education (Fuchs & Fuchs, 2006). When special education was first identified as a national priority, estimates of the prevalence of learning disabilities indicated that perhaps 2% of students in public schools would be classified as learning disabled. Today, well in excess of 5% of students in public schools are so classified, and that number seems to increase each year. According to a 2003 national survey, prevalence varies widely throughout the states, ranging from a low of 2.96% in Kentucky to a high of 9.46% in Rhode Island (Reschly et al., 2003). The discrepancy across states seems to be attributable to another problem with the definition, which is a lack of uniformity between state eligibility criteria. The results of the aforementioned survey revealed state-to-state differences in the requirements for IQ, psychological process disorders, achievement domains, exclusion criteria, and methods for determining discrepancy. Based on these discrepancies, a child receiving specialized services in one state may be deemed ineligible for services if they move across the state line.

Other problems with the LD definition have been noted as well. For example, children may be diagnosed as disabled in reading based on evaluation instruments that have poor validity. Further, evaluation and application of diagnostic criteria in the LD definition provide no guidance for instruction. In addition, the severe discrepancy model does not distinguish between reading deficits caused by poor instruction versus reading deficits caused by biologically based deficits (Vellutino et al., 2006).

Clearly, the need for clarification and revision of the definition and eligibility procedures for documenting learning disabilities is apparent. Through the discussion and debates of expert researchers and educators, response to intervention has risen to the top of the myriad of options for determining LD eligibility. However, many practitioners have not had direct experience with RTI because this option for eligibility is so recent. Further, few states have devised methods for implementation of this option, as the new federal regulations went into effect in August 2006.

WHY DID RTI EVOLVE?

In 1982, a National Research Council Study (Heller, Holtzman, & Messick, 1982) outlined three criteria on which special education classification should be based. The first criterion involves determining if the quality of instruction received in the general education environment is sufficient for adequate learning. The second criterion examines whether the special education program is appropriate and of value in improving student outcomes. Finally, the third criterion is that the evaluation process must be valid and meaningful. When all three criteria are achieved, special education placement is considered valid (Vaughn & Fuchs, 2003).

The study by Heller and colleagues (1982) began the momentum for use of responsiveness to instruction in eligibility determinations. This process had been used in two earlier studies (Bergan, 1977; Deno & Mirkin, 1977) that involved similar methodologies; one explored behavioral issues and the other focused on academics. In these studies, a definition of the problem was clearly established and measurable goals were developed based on the student's functioning level. An intervention plan was developed utilizing research-based interventions. Progress was monitored through curriculum-based assessment tools. Finally, decisions regarding continuation or dismissal of interventions were based on achievement of goals and benchmarks.

Over the next two decades, RTI would be heavily debated and researched. Numerous organizations, discussion panels, roundtables, and summits were convened to bring together experts from the field to make recommendations for policy changes (see Table 1.1). In 2001, President George W. Bush established the Commission on Excellence in Special Education (2002) to study special education issues and make recommendations

Table 1.1 Research and Policy Reports Supporting Response to Intervention

Reporting Organization	Date Published	Content of Report
National Institute for Child Health and Development (NIHCD) Studies	Ongoing	Concluded that IQ achievement discrepancy delays services to children. Supports early intervention services as provided through RTI.
National Reading Panel	2000	Outlined major components of reading.
National Research Council Panel on Minority Overrepresentation	2002	Emphasized importance of early identification and intervention for poor and minority children and youth. Made recommendations for LD eligibility criteria.
National Summit on Learning Disabilities	2001	Recommended Response to Intervention as the "most promising" method of LD identification.
President's Commission on Excellence in Special Education	2001	Recommended a focus on results and prevention in LD eligibility determination.

SOURCE: Batsche et al. (2006), Fuchs et al. (2005).

concerning how services might be improved. That commission issued a report that recommended early intervention and assessment practices that were closely linked to instruction. In summation, the commission strongly suggested changing LD eligibility criteria from a discrepancy model to a response to intervention model, which documents how a student suspected of having a learning disability responds to appropriate instruction. This RTI model is described in detail in the following section.

In 2002, the National Research Center on Learning Disabilities issued the *Common Ground Report*, which identified fourteen recommendations regarding identification, eligibility, and intervention for learning disabilities. The report was the product of leaders from eight national organizations coming together to form a consensus on their philosophies regarding LD. Marston (2005) compared the consensus statements to three sound RTI projects in order to determine if the RTI process fulfilled the requirements outlined in the *Common Ground Report*. He determined that RTI positively corresponded to each of the statements, making the process a viable option for LD determination. The consensus statements are listed in Table 1.2.

Table 1.2 Consensus Statements From the *Common Ground Report* of the National Research Center on Learning Disabilities (2002)

- Identification should include a student-centered, comprehensive evaluation and problem-solving approach that ensures students who have a specific learning disability are efficiently identified.
- The field should continue to advocate for the use of scientifically based practices. However, in areas where an adequate research base does not exist, data should be gathered on the success of promising practices.
- Regular education must assume active responsibility for delivery of high-quality instruction, research-based interventions, and prompt identification of individuals at risk while collaborating with special education and related services personnel.
- Schools and educators must have access to information about scientifically based practices and promising practices that have been validated in the settings where they are to be implemented.
- The ability-achievement discrepancy formula should not be used for determining eligibility.
- Students with specific learning disabilities require intensive, iterative (recursive), explicit scientifically based instruction that is monitored on an ongoing basis to achieve academic success.
- Students with specific learning disabilities require a continuum of intervention options through regular and special education across all grades and ages.
- Decisions on eligibility must be made through an interdisciplinary team, using informed clinical judgment, directed by relevant data, and based on student needs and strengths.
- Interventions must be timely and matched to the specific learning and behavioral needs of the student.
- An intervention is most effective when it is implemented consistently, with fidelity to its design, and at a sufficient level of intensity and duration.
- Based on an individualized evaluation and continuous progress monitoring, a student who has been identified as having a specific learning disability may need different levels of special education and related services under IDEA at various times during the school experience.

Reflection 1.2   **Who Determines Policy on LD Definition?**

As described previously, several national study groups have determined that RTI is an effective way to identify students with a learning disability. Both the Commission on Excellence in Education and the National Research Center on Learning Disabilities have weighed in and supported the RTI concept. However, this begs the question of who determines policy on LD definitions. One frequently overlooked fact is that each individual state, via rules and regulations from the state department of education, effectively sets the LD definition and the procedures whereby eligibility determinations may be made. Thus, one critical question for practitioners is: Has your state department of education begun the process of adjusting their rules, regulations, and procedures to accommodate the new rules and regulations that became effective in August 2006? The Web site for those federal rules and regulations is: www.ed.gov/idea.

WHAT IS RTI?

Response to Intervention is, simply put, a process of implementing high-quality, scientifically validated instructional practices based on learner needs, monitoring student progress, and adjusting instruction based on the student's response. When a student's response is dramatically inferior to that of his peers, the student may be determined to have a learning disability (Fuchs, 2003). The assumption is that failure to respond to otherwise effective instruction indicates the possible presence of a disabling condition. Interventions are most often divided into tiers of instruction. Although the RTI model seems relatively simple and straightforward, the actual implementation of the process requires much consideration and planning of the specific intricacies to make it valid, reliable, and feasible.

The two studies that formed the early research support for RTI (Bergan, 1977; Deno & Mirkin, 1977) were discussed previously. These studies varied in their RTI procedures; those variations have evolved into the problem-solving RTI model and the standard protocol RTI approach. It is important to understand both approaches in order to determine the most effective means of implementation.

In his research, Bergan (1977) utilized a problem-solving approach to address behavioral issues among students in special education. In this process, the behavioral problem was first defined and then measured as accurately as possible. The student's functioning and performance gap in comparison to peers was then established. The intervention team applied a problem-solving process to interpret the data and establish a goal for the student based on the performance of his or her peers. Next, the team designed an intervention plan based on scientifically validated practices for behavior change. Interventions designed specifically for that student were implemented over a period of time and progress was monitored frequently. Data collected from the ongoing progress monitoring was then evaluated and results were, again, compared to peer performance. Finally, the team used the data to make programming decisions for the student (Batsche, et al., 2006). Thus, the team-based "problem-solving approach" evolved based on this general design.

Deno and Mirkin (1977) implemented a different approach in their research. They utilized curriculum-based measurement, a technique that has been proven as an effective method for assessing a pupil's academic progress over time. They then developed an intervention plan to remediate certain reading difficulties among students with learning disabilities. In the growing RTI literature, this method became known as the "standard treatment protocol."

Although there are numerous similarities between the approaches used in these studies, there are some very important differences. Deno and

Mirkin utilized curriculum-based measures to establish benchmarks for student achievement. In this model, each student was essentially compared to his or her own prior performance. This is different from Bergan's problem-solving approach, which compares a pupil's performance to his or her peers. Further, the curriculum-based measures in the standard protocol approach were administered quite often, allowing for a constant adjustment of instruction based on student response. The team determined whether to discontinue, continue, adjust, or intensify instruction based on the student's responsiveness to the adjusted instruction (Kukic, Tilly, & Michelson, 2006).

| **Reflection 1.3** | **Your Use of Curriculum-Based Measurement** |

As you can tell from these initial studies on RTI, the standard treatment protocol is more heavily dependent on curriculum-based measurement than the problem-solving approach, although both incorporate curriculum-based measurement. What is your previous experience with curriculum-based measurement on a weekly, biweekly, or daily basis? Are you currently using such a progress-monitoring tool to follow students' academic growth in your class, or will you need to learn new skills in order to implement curriculum-based measurement?

Thus, from these original studies, two distinct RTI models emerged; the problem-solving model and the standard protocol model. Although the models exhibit similar structure, the processes involved in developing and evaluating the impact or efficacy of the educational interventions are quite different. In essence, the problem-solving approach involves the implementation of interventions designed for individual student needs. The standard protocol approach relies on interventions designed for small groups of students experiencing the same academic problem (e.g., reading comprehension). Both approaches require research-based interventions, ongoing progress monitoring, and measures to assure fidelity and integrity of the intervention and assessment (National Research Center on Learning Disabilities, 2005). In the remainder of this chapter, we will explore examples of each model, noting strengths and weaknesses for both.

THE PROBLEM-SOLVING APPROACH TO RTI

As previously stated, the problem-solving model involves individualized decision making and intervention implementation for each student. Problem-solving teams at the school or system level evaluate student data and make decisions about the need for interventions, the interventions to be used, and the amount of time allotted for each intervention (McCook, 2006). The problem-solving model has been replicated and refined in several school systems, including Minneapolis Public Schools and the Heartland Area Educational Agency in Iowa.

The Minneapolis Public Schools began formal implementation of the problem-solving model in 1992 (Marston, Muyskens, Lau, & Canter, 2003). Their problem-solving model is a sequential pattern of steps divided into three tiers or stages. They are:

Stage 1. Classroom Interventions: This stage is implemented by classroom teachers in general education classrooms. Teachers identify students who are experiencing difficulties, implement instructional strategies or modifications based on individual student needs, and begin to monitor the student's progress. Teachers gather information regarding strengths and specific weaknesses, previous strategies attempted and outcomes, any available screening data, student health, and other information from parents. If the teacher determines the intervention is not successful, the student is referred to Stage 2.

Stage 2. Problem-Solving Team Interventions: Student information is reviewed by a multidisciplinary team, which may include school psychologists, general education and special education teachers, reading specialists, and school administrators. The team considers whether other risk factors (language, poverty, cultural factors) are attributing to or causing the student's lack of progress. Interventions are reviewed and adjusted to more specifically address student needs. Teachers continue to monitor progress and adjust instruction. If teachers determine the student is not sufficiently responding to instruction, the student is referred to Stage 3.

Stage 3. Special Education Referral and Initiation of Due Process Procedures: The school district obtains parental consent and begins evaluation procedures for the student. The evaluation consists of a review of all information available on the student from Stages 1 and 2, including data on the student's response to interventions, direct observation, and the formulation of a means of obtaining cognitive, achievement, and adaptive behavior functioning. The team utilizes all available information to determine eligibility while considering the possible impact of risk factors such as culture, language, and socioeconomic status (Marston et al., 2003).

In 2002, the Minneapolis School District (approximately one hundred total schools) had implemented the problem-solving model in all K–8 schools and was in the training phase for all secondary schools. Outcome data revealed that the prevalence of students with high-incidence disabilities remained constant (7%) before and after implementation. Further, the achievement level of these students on the Minnesota Basic Standards Tests and the Minnesota State Special Education Goals was similar to that of students placed in special education using more traditional methods. Finally, the number of students referred to Stage 3 and placed in special education did not increase (Marston et al., 2003), nor was any decrease in placement noted. Instead, the placement rate remained stable at approximately 7% for the areas of LD and mild mental impairment.

A second example of the problem-solving model was implemented by the Heartland Area Educational Agency. That agency serves approximately 24% of students in the Iowa Public Schools. In 1990, the agency began implementation of a four-tiered problem-solving model. The transition to the problem-solving model involved a shift from traditional special education and general education resources to a seamless model of resource allocation. Similar to the Minnesota Public Schools problem-solving model, Heartland's model involved instruction and assessment at an individual student level (Tilley, 2003).

Tilley (2003) identified several "operational challenges" involved with the four-tiered, individually based system. These challenges included the fact that it is often not feasible to work with student problems at an individual level on a large scale. The resources required make the instructional process somewhat inefficient, especially when working with mild educational problems among large numbers of students. In the past three years, Heartland has shifted to a three-tiered model using the following tiers:

Tier One: Core Instructional Curriculum (all students involved)

Tier Two: Core Instruction and Supplemental Instructional Resources (students who need additional assistance—group or individual assistance)

Tier Three: Core Instructional and Intensive Resources (students who need intensive interventions and specialized resources on an individual basis)

Heartland defines their problem-solving model as "a process that includes an objective definition of student behavior problems or academic difficulties, systematic analysis of the student's problem and implementation of a planned systematic set of interventions" (Grimes & Kurns, 2003). Heartland incorporated "science into practice" by applying the scientific method in the decision-making process (Tilley, 2003). This process was applied at each intervention tier, utilizing four components (see following box).

Define the problem: What is the problem? Why is it happening?

The team looks at the gap between expected and actual student behavior or performance. Appropriate assessment and data analysis are used to distinguish specific problems and to attempt to rule out inappropriate instruction as the cause for this gap.

Develop a plan: What is going to be done about the problem?

Interventions are formulated based on student weaknesses and needs. Research-based strategies are key elements of the plan.

Implement the plan: Is the plan being implemented as intended?

The intervention is implemented as designed. Ongoing progress monitoring is used to evaluate intervention effectiveness.

Evaluate: Did the plan work as intended?

Data gathered throughout the implementation period are evaluated to determine the next course of action (Grimes & Kurns, 2003).

The multidisciplinary team utilizes this ongoing process to make appropriate decisions regarding instructional programming. Intensive support is provided through the Heartland Agency to each school involved in the project. This support most frequently takes the form of additional personnel such as school psychologists, educational consultants, social workers, and/or speech-language pathologists. Students who progress through each tier without making acceptable progress are considered for possible special education eligibility and placement (Jankowski, 2003).

Another important aspect of Heartland's model is teacher training. Teachers in all participating schools receive intensive training in research-based strategies and assessment. In addition, Heartland provides training on problem solving, team building, data collection, and data interpretation. Ongoing training and support have proven to be essential components of the model (Grimes & Kurns, 2003).

The Heartland Agency reports a significant reduction in special education placement rates among kindergarten through third graders. After implementation of the Heartland Early Literacy Project in coordination with the problem-solving model, thirty-nine participating schools reported the following results for the years 1999–2004 (Tilley, 2003):

- Forty-one percent reduction in special education initial placements in kindergarten
- Thirty-four percent reduction in special education initial placements in first grade

- Twenty-five percent reduction in special education initial placements in second grade
- Nineteen percent reduction in special education initial placements in third grade

As you might note, the reduction percentage of students eligible for special education did decline. However, we should note that in the Heartland Agency example, that reduction percentage was noted among students referred for all categories of special education, not merely learning disabilities.

THE STANDARD PROTOCOL RTI MODEL

The standard protocol model utilizes a set of standard research-based interventions usually implemented in two, three, or four tiers or levels. In contrast to the problem-solving model, the interventions occur in a natural progression from tier to tier, and are similar for all students experiencing the same learning problems rather than being specially designed for each individual student. There is a large body of research using standard protocol. In this section, we will explore several studies performed by leading researchers in the RTI field.

McMaster, Fuchs, Fuchs, and Compton (2003) implemented a standard protocol RTI to identify reading problems in eight metropolitan Nashville schools. Students in first-grade classrooms were taught reading using a standard curriculum and the usual reading materials. Students were then assessed using a "Rapid Letter Naming" test. The eight lowest performing students in each classroom were placed in groups where they were instructed with one of two research-based strategies. These two strategies were Peer-Assisted Learning Strategies (PALS), or "PALS + Fluency." First-grade PALS reading (Fuchs et al., 2001) is a peer-assisted instructional process whereby students tutor each other in a reciprocal fashion for some brief period each day. Developed by researchers at Vanderbilt University, PALS focuses on phonological awareness, beginning decoding, word recognition, and fluency. "PALS + Fluency" has an added focus on reading fluency and comprehension (McMaster et al., 2003, p. 9).

In this study, students received ongoing progress monitoring using nonword fluency probes from the Dynamic Indicators of Basic Early Literacy Skills (DIBELS; Good & Kaminski, 2001) and Dolch word probes. After seven weeks of instruction, students were classified as nonresponders if they scored 0.5 standard deviation below average readers on several criteria. Nonresponders were then placed in smaller groups where they received more intensive PALS, modified PALS, or tutoring for a period of thirteen weeks. Modified PALS places three modifications on the PALS design: fewer sounds and words are introduced at once and students work at their functioning level, the student serving as the "coach" models the sounds and words, and phonological awareness and decoding skills are emphasized more (McMaster et al., 2003, p. 9). In the PALS and modified PALS groups, interventions were provided by peers, as the program design dictates. In the tutoring groups, intervention was provided by a trained adult. Again, progress was monitored for each student biweekly. The study explored issues such as appropriate identification criteria and effective instructional strategies.

One of the most comprehensive studies of the standard treatment protocol for RTI was conducted by Vellutino et al. (2006) in suburban and rural schools in New York. This five-year longitudinal study explored the impact of kindergarten and first-grade interventions for children identified as at risk for reading disabilities. The initial sample of 1,373 children was assessed on letter-name knowledge at the beginning of kindergarten. Results of those assessments indicated that approximately 30% of the children were at risk for reading difficulties. Those at-risk students were then divided equally into treatment and control groups. The treatment group members were provided with a small-group (two or three children) early literacy intervention program throughout their kindergarten year. The intervention was provided by a certified teacher who had been trained on that curriculum by project staff. Students were pulled from the general education classroom for two thirty-minute sessions each week. Progress was monitored three times during the school year (December, March, and June). Initial results indicated a significant improvement in reading ability for the treatment group.

During the following year, researchers reassessed all students who had been members of the kindergarten treatment and control groups. Based on this assessment, 50% of the treatment group participants qualified as poor readers whereas 60% of the control group members were considered to be poor readers. All students identified as poor readers in first grade were either given individual tutoring by project teachers or the remediation normally provided by the school in the first-grade classroom. Progress was monitored for all students through the completion of their third-grade year. Results of the study revealed that of the students receiving kindergarten-only interventions or both kindergarten and first-grade interventions, 84% performed in the average range on reading measures by the end of third grade. This is a dramatic turnaround among these poor readers. Perhaps the most important finding of this study is the impact of early intervention for preventing reading disabilities.

Both of these studies involved identification of reading problems in children in third grade or younger. However, the standard treatment protocol model for RTI has also been used to prevent and identify mathematics disabilities. Fuchs et al., (2005) assessed the mathematics performance of children in forty-one first-grade classrooms (ten schools) using weekly curriculum-based measurement. The assessment tool consisted of twenty-five items related to math skills taught in the first-grade curriculum. Curriculum-based measurement scores were taken frequently and averaged across three to five weeks; based on those average scores, children who averaged less than eleven correct math problems were considered to be at risk for a mathematics disability.

These students were then placed into groups of two or three where they received tutoring and computer practice for a total of forty minutes, three times each week. An educational intervention involving tutoring based on the concrete-representational-abstract method for math instruction (Butler, Miller, Crehan, Babbitt, & Pierce, 2003; Cass, Cates, Smith, & Jackson, 2003; Mercer, Jordan, & Miller, 1996) was implemented until every member of the group achieved mastery or until every lesson on the topic had been taught. The method involves using manipulatives to provide for concept understanding. Seventeen topics were covered in up to sixty-six sessions (depending on mastery). Curriculum-based measures continued to be implemented throughout the study. The findings revealed improved performance on computation, concepts and applications, and completion of story problems. In these areas, at-risk students who received intervention outperformed students who received no intervention. Researchers also found that the growth of the at-risk tutored students was, on some measures, equal to or greater than students who were not considered to be at risk. Most important, the study revealed that early intervention in this case reduced the prevalence of math disability by an average of 35%.

In another study involving math performance, Fuchs et al. (2006) explored the effects of a curriculum called "Hot Math" (Fuchs, Fuchs, Prentice, Burch, & Paulsen, 2002) among third-grade students. Tier One involved Hot Math whole-class instruction in forty general education classrooms located in thirteen schools. Instruction was implemented two or three times each week for sixteen weeks, with each session lasting twenty-five to forty minutes. Students who scored lowest after this intervention were assigned to Tier Two Hot Math tutoring. This intervention occurred three times each week in twenty- to thirty-minute sessions for thirteen weeks. Groups composed of two to four students received this instruction together; a student was considered to be unresponsive to instruction if his or her daily performance was one standard deviation below the performance levels of the norm scores in the assessment. Thus, in this study, a student's performance was based on multiple measures and varied depending on how many tiers students participated in. Overall, the study revealed vast improvement on all measures for the

Table 1.3 Strengths and Weaknesses of Problem-Solving and Standard Protocol RTIs

Model	Strengths	Weaknesses
Problem-Solving Model	• Decisions based on individual student needs • Allows more flexibility in choices of interventions and allocation of resources	• Dealing with learner problems at an individual level can become time consuming • Requires teachers and team members to have vast knowledge and expertise in research-based strategies
Standard Protocol Model	• Clear scientific process in literature for strategies and assessment • Standard interventions in place and readily available to students in need • Structured progression between tiers	• Less flexibility with choice of interventions (one size doesn't fit all) • May require additional staff, depending on available resources

majority of students receiving any level of intervention. Unresponsiveness in problem solving for students receiving only traditional math instruction was an alarming 86%–100%. Unresponsiveness for students receiving both tiers of intervention was 12%–26%. This study illustrated that the RTI model had a substantial impact on reducing the number of children at risk for math disability in third grade.

FINAL THOUGHTS

With the release of final IDEA regulations in August 2006, it is expected that many, if not all, states will incorporate some form of RTI into their policies and procedures. However, those regulations do not propose or recommend any specific RTI model. In fact, those regulations do not require implementation of any RTI procedure at all. Rather, those regulations allow RTI as an eligibility procedure for documentation of learning disabilities. The relevant section of those regulations is presented in the following box (see www.ed.gov/idea and look under "Changes in Initial Evaluation or Reevaluation"). According to that source, the IDEA legislation of 2004 includes the following provision.

> **Establishes procedures for evaluating a child suspected of having a specific learning disability.**
>
> Notwithstanding Section 607(b), when determining whether a child has a specific learning disability as defined in Section 602:
>
> An LEA shall not be required to take into consideration whether a child has a severe discrepancy between achievement and intellectual ability in oral expression, listening comprehension, written expression, basic reading skill, reading comprehension, mathematical calculation, or mathematical reasoning.
>
> An LEA may use a process that determines if the child responds to scientific, research-based intervention as a part of the evaluation procedures.
>
> (614(b)(6))

As you can see, this provision eliminates the requirement for a discrepancy calculation, but it does not explicitly prohibit the use of discrepancies. Further, this provision gives no guidance on which type of RTI—standard treatment protocol or problem-solving model—should be implemented.

Although the research base on RTI is broad in some areas, such as reading instruction and interventions for young children, there are many unanswered questions about implementation of RTI. Educators are left with the dilemma of working out the specifics for efficient, cost-effective implementation while providing the desired benefit of early intervention and appropriate disability identification. The remainder of this book will address these issues and provide guidance for effective implementation.

For planning purposes, it may be beneficial for a school or school district to examine current instructional procedures. Appendix A presents a "Needs Assessment" that focuses on many aspects of RTI that are discussed in subsequent chapters. This form may be used as is or adapted as school district personnel deem necessary to assist in your planning as you move into RTI.

REFERENCES

Batsche, G., Elliott, J., Graden, J. L., Grimes, J., Kovaleski, J. F., Prasse, D., et al. (2006). *Response to intervention: Policy considerations and implementation* (4th ed.). Alexandria, VA: National Association of State Directors of Special Education, Inc.

Bergan, J. R. (1977). *Behavioral consultation*. Columbus, OH: Charles E. Merrill.

Bradley, R., Danielson, L., & Doolittle, J. (2005). Response to intervention. *Journal of Learning Disabilities, 38*(6), 485–486.

Butler, F. M., Miller, S. P., Crehan, K., Babbitt, B., & Pierce, T. (2003). Fraction instruction for students with mathematics disabilities: Comparing two teaching sequences. *Learning Disabilities Research and Practice, 18,* 99–111.

Cass, M., Cates, D., Smith, M., & Jackson, C. (2003). Effects of manipulative instruction on solving area and perimeter problems by students with learning disabilities. *Learning Disabilities Research and Practice, 18,* 112–120.

Deno, S., & Mirkin, P. (1977). *Data-based program modification.* Minneapolis, MN: Leadership Training Institute for Special Education.

Fletcher, J. M., Denton, C., & Francis, D. J. (2005). Validity of alternative approaches for the identification of learning disabilities: Operationalizing unexpected underachievement. *Journal of Learning Disabilities, 38,* 545–552.

Fuchs, L. S. (2003). Assessing intervention responsiveness: Conceptual and technical issues. *Learning Disabilities Research and Practice, 18*(3), 172–186.

Fuchs, L. S., Compton, D. L., Fuchs, D., Paulsen, K., Bryant, J., & Hamlett, C. L. (2005). Responsiveness to intervention: Preventing and identifying mathematics disability. *TEACHING Exceptional Children, 37*(4), 60–63.

Fuchs, D., & Fuchs, L. S. (2005). Responsiveness-to-intervention: A blueprint for practitioners, policymakers, and parents. *Teaching Exceptional Children, 38*(1), 57–61.

Fuchs, D., & Fuchs, L. S. (2006). Introduction to Response to Intervention: What, why, and how valid is it? *Reading Research Quarterly, 41*(1), 93–98.

Fuchs, L. S., Fuchs, D., Hamlett, C. L., Hope, S. K., Hollenbeck, K. N., Capizzi, A., et al. (2006). Extending responsiveness to intervention to math problem-solving at third grade. *TEACHING Exceptional Children, 38*(4), 59–63.

Fuchs, L. S., Fuchs, D., Prentice, K., Burch, M., & Paulsen, K. (2002). Hot Math: Promoting mathematical problem solving among third-grade students with disabilities. *TEACHING Exceptional Children, 31*(1), 70–73.

Fuchs, D., Fuchs, L. S., Thompson, A., Svenson, E., Yen, L., Al Otaiba, S., et al. (2001). Peer-assisted learning strategies in reading: Extension for kindergarten, first grade, and high school. *Remedial and Special Education, 22,* 15–21.

Gersten, R., & Dimino, J. A. (2006). RTI (Response to Intervention): Rethinking special education for students with reading difficulties (yet again). *Reading Research Quarterly, 41*(1), 99–108.

Good, R. H., & Kaminski, R. A. (Eds.), (2001). *Dynamic indicators of basic early literacy skills* (5th ed.). Eugene, OR: Institute for the Development of Educational Achievement.

Grimes, J., & Kurns, S. (2003, December). *An intervention-based system for addressing NCLB and IDEA expectations: A multiple tiered model to ensure every child learns.* Paper presented at the National Research Center on Learning Disabilities Responsiveness-to-Intervention Symposium, Kansas City, MO

Heller, K. A., Holtzman, W. H., & Messick, S. (1982). *Placing children in special education: A strategy for equity.* Washington, DC: National Academy Press.

Individuals With Disabilities Education Act of 2004. (2004). Federal Register 71, pp. 46539–46845. Retrieved August 30, 2006, from www.ed.gov/policy/speced/guid/idea2004.html

Jankowski, E. A. (2003, Fall). Heartland Area Education Agency's problem solving model: An outcomes-driven special education paradigm. *Rural Special Education Quarterly.* Retrieved July 25, 2006, from www.findarticles.com/p/articles

Kukic, S., Tilly, D., & Michelson, L. (Presenters). (2006). *Addressing the needs of students with learning difficulties through the Response to Intervention (RtI) strategies.* Retrieved January 26, 2007, from the National Association of State Directors of Special Education, Inc., Web site: http://www.nasdse.org/publications.cfm

Marston, D. (2005). Tiers of intervention in responsiveness to intervention: Prevention outcomes and learning disabilities identification patterns. *Journal of Learning Disabilities, 38*(6), 539–544.

Marston, D., Muyskens, P., Lau, M., & Canter, A. (2003). Problem-solving model for decision making with high-incidence disabilities: The Minneapolis experience. *Learning Disabilities Research & Practice, 18*(3), 187–200.

Mastropieri, M. A., & Scruggs, T. W. (2005). Feasibility and consequences of Response to Intervention: Examination of the issues and scientific evidence as a model for the identification of individuals with learning disabilities. *Journal of Learning Disabilities, 38*(6), 525–531.

McCook, J. E. (2006). *The RTI guide: Developing and implementing a model in your schools.* Horsham, PA: LRP Publications.

McMaster, K. L., Fuchs, D., Fuchs, L. S., & Compton, D. L. (2003, December). *Responding to nonresponders: An experimental field trial of identification and intervention methods.* Paper presented at the National Research Center on Learning Disabilities Responsiveness-to-Intervention Symposium, Kansas City, MO.

Mercer, C. D., Jordan, L., & Miller, S. P. (1996). Constructivistic math instruction for diverse learners. *Learning Disabilities Research and Practice, 11,* 147–156.

National Research Center on Learning Disabilities (2002). *Common ground report.* Reston, VA: Author.

National Research Center on Learning Disabilities (2005). *Core concepts of RTI.* Retrieved July 25, 2006, from www.nrcld.org

President's Commission on Excellence in Special Education (2002). *A new era: Revitalizing special education for children and their families.* Retrieved July 26, 2006, from www.ed.gov/inits/commissionsboards/index.html

Reschly, D. J., Hosp, J. L., & Schmied, C. M. (2003, August 20). *And miles to go: State SLD requirements and authoritative recommendations.* Retrieved July 20, 2006, from www.nrcld.org, pp. 3–10.

Scruggs, T. W., & Mastropieri, M. A. (2002). On babies and bathwater: Addressing the problems of identification of learning disabilities. *Learning Disability Quarterly, 25*(2), 155–168.

Siegel, L. S. (1989). IQ is irrelevant to the definition of learning disabilities. *Journal of Learning Disabilities, 22,* 469–486.

Tilley, W. D. (2003, December). *How many tiers are needed for successful prevention and early intervention? Heartland Area Education Agency's evolution from four to three tiers.* Paper presented at the National Research Center on Learning Disabilities Responsiveness-to-Intervention Symposium, Kansas City, MO.

U.S. Office of Education. (1977). *Assistance to states for education of handicapped children: Procedures for evaluating specific learning disabilities.* Federal Register 42, pp. 65082–65085.

Vaughn, S., & Fuchs, L. S. (2003). Redefining learning disabilities as inadequate response to instruction: The promise and potential problems. *Learning Disabilities Research & Practice, 18*(3), 137–146.

Vaughn, S., Linan-Thompson, S., & Hickman, P. (2003). Response to treatment as a means of identifying students with reading/learning disabilities. *Exceptional Children, 69*(4), 391–409.

Vellutino, F. R., Scanlon, D. M., Sipay, E. R., Small, S., Chen, R., et al. (1996). Cognitive profiles of difficult to remediate and readily remediated poor readers: Early intervention as a vehicle for distinguishing between cognition and experiential deficits as basic cause of specific reading disability. *Journal of Educational Psychology, 88,* 601–638.

Vellutino, F. R., Scanlon, D. M., Small, S., & Fanuele, D. P. (2006). Response to intervention as a vehicle for distinguishing between children with and without reading disabilities: Evidence for the role of kindergarten and first-grade interventions. *Journal of Learning Disabilities, 39*(2), 157–169.

Ysseldyke, J. (2005). Assessment and decision making for students with learning disabilities: What if this is as good as it gets? *Learning Disability Quarterly, 28,* 125–128.

2

Implementation of a Standard Treatment Protocol Response to Intervention

William N. Bender and Cara Shores

In the RTI literature, it seems that most researchers have supported the standard treatment protocol as the RTI option of choice. This standard treatment protocol, as described previously, involves several separate educational interventions, progressing in intensity over time, prior to classification as learning disabled (Fuchs & Fuchs, 2005; Mellard, Byrd, Johnson, Tollefson, & Boesche, 2004). Thus, in contrast to the discrepancy procedure, which is dependent on a child's performance on "one time" assessments of academic achievement, the standard treatment protocol involves actually exposing a child to educational interventions and monitoring progress repeatedly to see how he or she responds. Under normal conditions, these systematic interventions with rigorous progress monitoring would be expected to result in academic growth. In the absence of such academic growth after several well-documented instructional interventions, a learning disability is assumed to exist under the new RTI procedures (Fuchs & Fuchs, 2006; Marston, 2005).

In the discussions available in the professional literature, a three-tiered system involving three separate interventions is typically recommended (Fuchs & Fuchs, 2006; Gersten & Dimino, 2006; Marston, Muyskens, Lau, & Canter, 2003; Mastropieri & Scruggs, 2005; National Joint Committee on Learning Disabilities [NJCLD], 2005; Vaughn, Linan-Thompson, & Hickman, 2003; Vellutino et al., 1996). Some suggest that the three tiers may be considered primary, secondary, and tertiary interventions, with the first tier focused populationwide, the second tier focused on more intensive smaller group work, and the third tier individually focused (Mellard et al., 2004). Although not universal, this three-tiered approach seems to be the most prevalent model; we will use this relatively standard model in this text. Figure 2.1 presents a three-tiered pyramid that may serve as a basis for understanding RTI.

Note that in Tier One of this pyramid (see Figure 2.1), most students experiencing educational difficulty (perhaps 80% of those students) should receive instruction that alleviates the problem without further assistance. Also, as noted in this pyramid, the first tier involves interventions that take place in the general education class. Tier Two is also a general education responsibility, but it involves a more intensive intervention and perhaps more intensive progress monitoring. Also, Tier Two typically involves some outside assistance from other teachers and/or experts in subject areas (e.g., the reading specialist at the school). The educational difficulties of some students (perhaps 15%) can be alleviated at this level. Finally, as shown here, Tier Three is typically described as the final intervention level; students enter Tier Three after the educators at the school determine that a learning

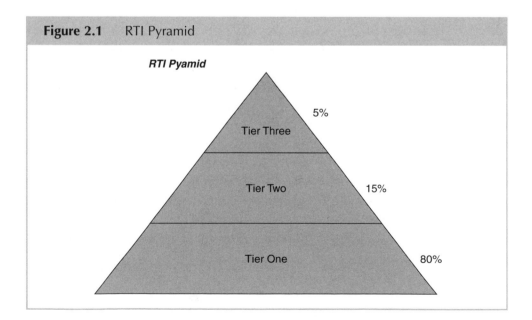

Figure 2.1 RTI Pyramid

disability exists. According to this model, only 5% or so of students would need to receive services in Tier Three.

Of course, as noted previously, various states have developed similar pyramids involving many more tiers. In order to demonstrate a different pyramid, Appendix B presents a four-tier model that is utilized by the State of Georgia as the basic RTI intervention model. Various states will choose different models; some include five or even six levels in the RTI process. The three-tier model, however, is more common across the states. Therefore, we will present several examples in this and subsequent chapters illustrating how a three-tier RTI model might be implemented across several grade levels.

EXAMPLE ONE: LEARNING NEW WORDS: FIRST GRADE

Caleb is in the first grade, and is heavily involved in learning to read. The teacher, Ms. Thompson, noticed during the first couple of weeks of school that Caleb is struggling in reading, and in particular that he doesn't seem to be mastering new vocabulary words as quickly as he should. When Ms. Thompson checked the screening assessment in reading, which was administered during the last month of Caleb's kindergarten year, she verified that Caleb was in the lower 20% of students on that assessment. Given these concerns, Ms. Thompson implemented a Tier One intervention for Caleb to ascertain how he responds to intervention.

In the first tier of the RTI procedure, the general education teacher, upon first suspecting a learning disability, is expected to implement a scientifically validated reading curriculum across a period of several weeks. This intervention typically takes place in the general education class, and is primarily the responsibility of the general education teacher. In some cases, this intervention may involve nothing more than an effort to more accurately monitor Caleb's progress while continuing the classwide instruction in which he is already participating. In other cases, a separate educational intervention may be selected.

Although Ms. Thompson would typically be primarily responsible for this Tier One intervention, it does not mean other educators have to be excluded. For example, Ms. Thompson should feel free to implement such instruction with a co-teaching partner or her paraprofessional. In this example, Ms. Thompson has been using a basal reader and each lesson in that text does focus on phonemic skills and word attack skills for whole class instruction. Therefore, in this case, she chooses not to implement an entirely new curriculum but, rather, to more closely monitor Caleb's progress in the curriculum currently in use for the whole class. Specifically, Ms. Thompson would monitor Caleb's progress in recognition of new vocabulary terms in isolation, perhaps on a weekly basis (Fuchs & Fuchs, 2005). She will also chart Caleb's individual progress. If Caleb does not progress in the Tier One intervention, he will be placed in a second-tier reading intervention, which should involve a more intensive reading program for another period of several weeks.

Tier One Intervention

Note that in conducting the Tier One standard protocol intervention, the general education teacher is expected to generate repetitive assessments to depict the child's response to the educational intervention over time (Fuchs & Fuchs, 2005, 2006; Gersten & Dimino, 2006; Marston, 2005). The teacher then charts those academic scores of reading skill to present a picture of the child's learning progress. For example, the data in Figure 2.2 represents weekly progress monitoring for Caleb. In order to generate these scores, Caleb was presented with a list of vocabulary terms at the first-grade reading level and asked to read those terms at the end of each week for one grading period. Ms. Thompson counted the number of words read correctly from that list of first-grade words in one minute. For Grade Level 1, Caleb would normally be expected to read fifteen to nineteen words correctly in one minute; any student who could not read fifteen words correctly in one minute would be judged to have a significant reading difficulty. In this example, the student's progress in word reading was monitored over a period of eight weeks.

Reflection 2.1	What Advantages Result From This Additional Work?

Teachers may initially believe that providing Tier One interventions and appropriate progress monitoring will take a great deal of time. You may wish to reflect on the following questions. In the Tier One interventions, what types of additional work is the general education teacher undertaking? How might the teacher find time for that progress monitoring? How much time each week would this individualized assessment take? Once a system of progress monitoring is implemented, could paraprofessionals and/or co-teachers be utilized for that work? Would the generation of these data on word reading over an eight-week period show parents that the teacher is heavily involved and spending extra time with Caleb? Take just a few moments and list other advantages you can see to taking this bit of additional time on Caleb's reading problem.

As shown in Figure 2.2, Caleb was not progressing in the first tier of the RTI process, despite the fact that the teacher used a scientifically validated reading curriculum (as is mandated currently under the federal

Figure 2.2   Tier One Intervention: Words Read Correctly Each Week by Caleb

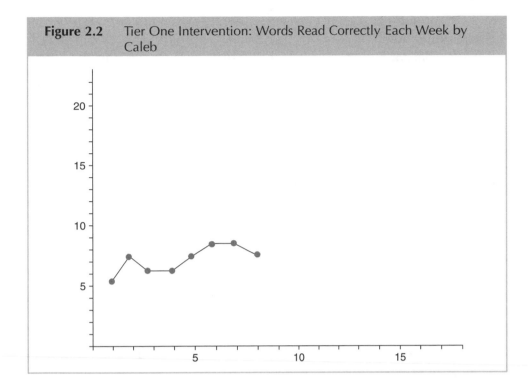

No Child Left Behind legislation), and that the teacher and paraprofessional implemented this curriculum with careful attention to the instructions on how to teach using those materials. In short, Caleb should have responded to that intervention, but the data show that he did not.

One issue in making such a summative statement, however, involves the question of "how much progress is enough?" In order to address that issue, the literature on RTI has reported on the "slope of the learning curve." Thus, learning should be documented by a considerable upward progression of academic behavior on charts such as the one presented in Figure 2.2. The term "slope" appears frequently in the literature, and although various guidelines are provided for an appropriate "slope of academic success," it is clear from the chart in Figure 2.2 that Caleb was not progressing sufficiently in his recognition of words.

However, another issue must also be discussed. The No Child Left Behind legislation, which mandated appropriate use of scientifically validated curricula, was intended to ensure that every child has an appropriate opportunity to learn to read. One question, therefore, involves how a teacher or paraprofessional may implement the reading curriculum for Caleb. In short, did the teacher or paraprofessional teach the curricular materials in the correct fashion, according to the instructor's teaching manual, which would thereby allow the student to learn the content? This issue is commonly referred to with the term "treatment fidelity" or "instructional fidelity."

When placement decisions on individual children are concerns, documentation of the treatment fidelity becomes necessary to protect the child from inappropriate placement. In this example, although Ms. Thompson is confident that she implemented the instruction correctly, others might ask questions, such as

> "Did Ms. Thompson implement the curricula in a way that was consistent with the way the curricula was utilized in the scientific validation studies and in accordance with the implementation guidelines for that particular reading program?"

> "Did she use the lessons for an appropriate number of minutes per day?"

> "Did Caleb have an appropriate opportunity to learn reading in Ms. Thompson's class, and how can that be documented?"

Beyond the general suggestion to provide professional development on various curricula (Fuchs & Fuchs, 2005), the available literature on RTI has not dealt with this implementation issue adequately. We would like to recommend that, during the RTI process, teachers go to some lengths to ensure that their instructional use of a particular curriculum is in accordance with the scientifically validated implementation guidelines. Although this may sound daunting at first glance, this assurance should be relatively simple to achieve.

The issue of scientifically validated instruction is really a twofold issue:

1. Is a scientifically validated reading, math, or subject area curriculum being utilized?

2. Is the teacher or paraprofessional implementing the curriculum in a scientifically validated manner?

First, it is clear from federal legislation that schools should proactively select their reading, math, and other curricula based on independent (i.e., not publisher supported) scientific validation studies. Many reading, math, and other curricula are validated in the scientific educational literature; selection of such curricula should be relatively simple. Of course, guidance may be provided here by curriculum coordinators or directors of instruction at the school district level and subject area experts from the state department of instruction.

A trickier issue is the second one mentioned previously: the documentation that teachers and paraprofessionals utilize the curricula appropriately in accordance with the procedures recommended by the publishers. To address this issue during the RTI procedure, educators should utilize actual observations of the teacher's or paraprofessional's instruction in order to document instructional consistency with the recommendations made in the selected curriculum (Mellard, Byrd, Johnson, Tollefson, & Boesche, 2004). There are several reasons that observations of instruction, rather than merely self-evaluation checklists concerning instruction, should be used. First, teachers are observed frequently by school administrators and/or master teachers throughout the school year. This can provide one way to document fidelity of instruction and appropriate use of a scientifically validated curriculum. Next, observation during instruction can provide additional insight into a student's learning. Holding one such observation during the reading instruction that involves Caleb should be relatively easy to do. Such an observation would then serve the twofold purpose of:

1. Documenting that Caleb was provided the opportunity to learn those reading skills during the RTI intervention, and

2. Providing an opportunity for an educator other than Caleb's primary teacher to observe how Caleb responds during the actual instructional lessons.

In every observation of instruction, administrators should be encouraged to note that the subject area curriculum was implemented in a manner consistent with the recommendations of the publishers of that curriculum. While this observation requirement may seem quite cumbersome, the fact is that a child's eligibility for services will depend on his or her response to intervention; schools have an obligation to document appropriate use of the curriculum when weighty questions such as "Does Caleb have a learning disability?" depend on appropriate curriculum implementation.

Observations of instruction take place all the time in public schools. These are required in various school-improvement programs, such as "Learning Focused Schools." Also, numerous "Initial Teacher" or "Beginning Teacher" programs involve periodic observation of teaching skill. Given the importance of scientifically validated instruction in the RTI process, at least one such observation of the Tier One instruction involving Caleb should be undertaken in order to ensure that the scientifically validated reading program was correctly administered.

Recommending observations during the RTI process may be controversial. Although administrators are required to observe teachers' instructional competence, having such observations completed by others (e.g., master teachers, special education consultants) can be viewed as problematic. Further, observations of instruction, in many cases, make even the most effective teachers somewhat uncomfortable. However, in this RTI instance, the observation is focused differently than the traditional administrator's observation of teachers. For the RTI process, the observation should be completed to address two main questions:

1. Is this instructional program implemented as it was intended to be implemented?

2. Are important anecdotal aspects of the student's learning noted, which may inform or clarify either the eligibility decision or the instructional program (e.g., learning style, learning preferences, performance)?

Emphasizing this rather limited focus for the RTI observation should assist teachers in becoming more comfortable with this process.

Reflection 2.2	Can These Observations of Instructional Fidelity Be Advantageous?

The text mentions several advantages of using observations during RTI to document fidelity to the curriculum. Can you think of other advantages? Take a moment and list several additional advantages of the use of observations during the RTI process.

Perhaps at this point it would be beneficial to review several of the guidelines mentioned in the model Tier One RTI process previously described. Table 2.1 presents these guidelines. As you read through these guidelines, you should reflectively review the example and note how these guidelines were applied in that example.

Tier Two Intervention

Typically, Tier Two interventions involve a more intensive instructional program for an additional period of several weeks; the mandate under No Child Left Behind requires implementation of a research-based approach to instruction. Given that mandate, the general education teacher should, at this point, consult with special education teachers, reading specialists, or school psychologists to identify and implement a program that is specific to the academic delay shown by the child and supported by the scientific literature.

Although consultation for selection of the Tier One intervention may be considered optional, consultation regarding Caleb's reading curriculum and design for Tier Two intervention should be considered mandatory. In Caleb's case, that program should involve various phonemic-based

Table 2.1 Guidelines for Tier One Intervention

1. When a teacher suspects a problem, he or she must obtain an appropriate score on a general screening measure (typically in either reading or math), or administer such a measure to get a general picture of the child's academic ability in comparison with other children.

2. When the screening score indicates an academic score in the bottom 20% to 25% of the population, a Tier One intervention must be initiated (Fuchs & Fuchs, 2005). Tier One interventions are undertaken in the general education classroom, and are the responsibility of the general education teacher.

3. Tier One interventions may involve educational curricula and procedures that the teacher has either implemented for the entire class or for a subgroup of students within the class.

4. Tier One interventions may be implemented by the general education teacher without consultation, as these are a function of the general education classroom.

5. During the reading instructional lesson for the student, the reading teacher or school administrator should observe Ms. Thompson teach reading, and should prepare a set of notes from that observation attesting to the implementation of the reading curriculum in a manner commensurate with the recommended teaching procedures.

6. Because Tier One interventions are a function of the general education classroom, these interventions are available to all students. Thus, implementation of Tier One interventions do not require specific notification of parents, although teachers would typically be expected to communicate with all parents regarding the general progress of their children.

7. Tier One interventions should result in a minimum of six data points or six assessments of academic progress, which allow the teacher to determine how the student responded to intervention a minimum of six times over a specified time period, which may be from six to ten weeks. This should involve assessments at least once a week.

reading activities that would be expected to prepare Caleb for improved oral reading of words in isolation.

Fuchs and Fuchs (2005) suggest that Tier Two intervention should involve intensive small-group instruction involving no more than one adult and two or three children. In such small-group instruction, teachers can individually attend to the reading skills of each individual child and can individually diagnose reading difficulties much more accurately than in whole class instruction. Although the general education teacher may implement the Tier Two intervention, others may implement this intervention as well. For example, the reading teacher may be able to add Caleb to a reading group for some intensive small-group instruction for thirty to forty-five minutes daily for a period of weeks.

The available literature on RTI suggests that Tier Two interventions must check the student's response to intervention over time; most researchers suggest that a six to eight week period is necessary to assess the impact of the Tier Two intervention (Fuchs & Fuchs, 2006; Fuchs, Fuchs, & Compton, 2004; Marston, 2005; Mastropieri & Scruggs, 2005; Vaughn, Linan-Thompson, & Hickman, 2003). However, the number of weeks of intervention is not as critical as the number of data points on which one's decisions are based, so the length of time in Tier Two is related to how frequently Caleb's reading progress is monitored.

In the literature, various researchers have recommended different frequencies of time for progress monitoring on the Tier Two intervention. For example, Fuchs and Fuchs (2005) recommended weekly progress monitoring in Tier Two, whereas Vaughn and her colleagues (2003) used a progress-monitoring system that documented progress twice per month. In contrast, we recommend daily progress monitoring for the second tier intervention. We believe that daily progress monitoring is truly the "best practice" in education today. The literature on curriculum-based measurement documents that very frequent monitoring of pupil progress results in enhanced instruction (Deno, 2003). Further, many scientifically validated curricula that are currently on the market present the option for daily monitoring of pupil progress. Thus, why would any teacher, in implementing RTI for eligibility purposes, fail to use a daily performance measure for this intensive, Tier Two intervention? Again, we advocate daily progress monitoring in Tier Two interventions because we believe that setting a higher standard for pupil progress monitoring in Tier Two is desirable; simply put, a student's educational future may depend on this level of the RTI process.

With that preference stated, we acknowledge that some curricula offer the option of twice a week or weekly monitoring of pupil progress; weekly monitoring has been recommended by others in the field (Fuchs & Fuchs, 2005). Therefore, progress monitoring on a weekly or twice weekly basis should be considered acceptable.

For the Tier Two intervention, based on discussions with the reading teacher, Ms. Thompson chose to let Caleb participate with that reading teacher who was using the *Reading Mastery Reading Program,* a direct instruction reading program that has been scientifically validated in a repeated series of studies. Thus, Caleb received intensive reading instruction for thirty-five minutes each day in a small group, and his progress was monitored during this intervention. Ms. Thompson and the reading teacher decided to chart Caleb's progress for part of the next grading period in that intensive reading instruction. Figure 2.3 presents a chart of daily performance of Caleb's progress in reading first-grade words in a one-minute timed period for his second tier intervention. Note that these data are presented based on daily progress monitoring over an eighteen-day period.

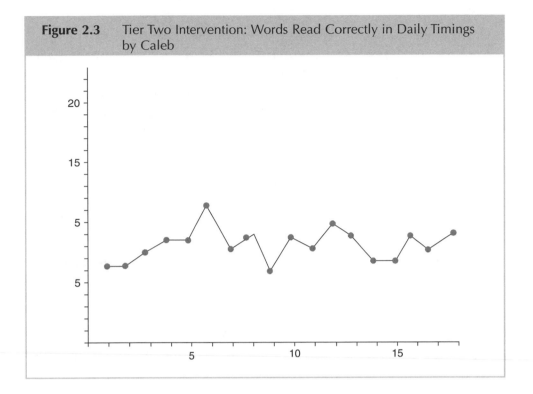

Figure 2.3 Tier Two Intervention: Words Read Correctly in Daily Timings by Caleb

Daily monitoring for three to four weeks is more effective than weekly monitoring over eight weeks because the former results in eighteen data points on which to base one's decision, whereas the latter results in only eight data points.

The instruction offered to Caleb during the Tier Two intervention should be monitored concerning the appropriateness of the instruction. The school administrator, the reading consultant, or the special educator should be used to observe the reading instruction for Caleb in Tier Two and make some notes as to the appropriateness of the instruction provided and the scientific validation of the curriculum utilized. Ideally, the person doing this observation should not be the same person who conducted the validation of instruction observation for Tier One; this would result in a third educator carefully observing not only the instruction presented but also Caleb's response to that instruction on a first-hand basis. Note that in the RTI procedure, these individuals will eventually be meeting with Caleb's parents and discussing the possibility of a special education placement for Caleb. Thus, these observations can provide several instructional personnel some opportunities to get to know Caleb.

Although some may consider this observation to be cumbersome and time consuming, this observation process is essential to the RTI process because one possible result is the documentation of a disability on the part of the child. Both Caleb and his parents deserve to know that various school personnel have done an appropriate job in instructing Caleb prior to documentation of a learning disability. We believe that multiple observations of Caleb's reading skill will indicate that the school personnel have made an extensive effort to meet the requirements of RTI. Thus, these observations will likely enhance the meeting with Caleb's parents.

It is important to point out that when implementing the RTI process as the main eligibility mechanism for documenting a learning disability, it is quite likely that these other individuals such as the special education teacher or the school psychologist will not spend nearly as much time testing Caleb as they would have under the older discrepancy procedure. Therefore, these individuals will have more time for conducting these observations of Caleb's instruction and how Caleb responds to that instruction.

The data in Figure 2.3 demonstrate that even in an intensive phonemically based reading program, Caleb was not progressing in his ability to read first-grade words in isolation. At this point, two separate interventions have been implemented for Caleb; each has shown that Caleb does not respond positively to these scientifically based interventions.

Again, a statement of guidelines for Tier Two interventions may be helpful. Note that these are merely guidelines and not requirements. However, we believe that these represent one effective way to document Tier Two Response to Intervention.

Tier Three Intervention

One would hope that intensive interventions of this nature result in documented progress for most students. However, some students such as Caleb might not benefit even from these intensive interventions. Pending a lack of sufficient growth during the Tier Two intervention, the child's team would meet and consider placing the child in special education. At this point, it would certainly be advantageous for various members who had actually observed Caleb during an instructional period to share their observations of his learning challenges. Parents should certainly be involved and, when practical, children themselves should be involved in this educational planning meeting. At this meeting, Caleb's eligibility for special education services as a child with a learning disability would be determined based on his failure to respond to two educationally sound interventions. This meeting and subsequent educational treatments would represent the third tier of the RTI process. The expectation noted from the RTI literature suggests that interventions in Tier Three would involve one-to-one instruction specifically targeted to the reading problems noted (Mellard, et al., 2004).

One question involves how many students with learning disabilities might be identified using this RTI process. Of course, the answer depends on the reading instructional procedures used, the quality of instruction,

Table 2.2 Guidelines for Tier Two Intervention

1. When the Tier One intervention is deemed unsuccessful, the special and general education teachers should briefly discuss the student's problem and select an intensive curriculum that addresses his specific reading problem. Other teachers might be involved if placements in a specialized reading program are considered, for example. These individuals should likewise make a determination as to who should implement this intensive instruction and how often.

2. Tier Two interventions that are undertaken in the general education classroom are either the responsibility of the general education teacher or his or her co-teacher or inclusion teacher. Interventions that involve the child's placement into another class must involve parental notification, parental permission, and hopefully parental participation in this meeting.

3. Tier Two interventions must be intensive interventions, involving a teacher and a small group of students in the instructional process. These interventions should be offered each day, or a minimum of four days each week.

4. During the Tier 2 reading instructional lesson, the reading teacher or school administrator should observe the reading lesson and, again, prepare a set of notes from that observation attesting to the implementation of the Tier 2 reading curriculum in a manner commensurate with the recommended teaching procedures.

5. Implementation of Tier Two interventions should involve specific notification of parents, because intensive instruction that is not typically offered to all children is being implemented for the student suspected of having a learning disability.

6. As noted previously, prior to a Tier Two intervention, the general education teacher should briefly consult with some other educator with particular expertise in the type of problem demonstrated by the student. This may be a special education teacher, school psychologist, reading teacher, curriculum coordinator for reading, or other specialist, but prior to implementing Tier Two interventions, some specialist must become involved.

7. Tier Two interventions should result in a minimum of twenty data points or twenty assessments of academic progress that allow the teacher to determine how the student responded to intervention a minimum of twenty times over a specified time period. The intervention itself may last from twenty days to up to ten weeks. This should involve assessments at least twice a week.

and many other factors. Still, the existing research give some clues to this question. A number of studies have been implemented, although these studies involved different lengths of time in Tier One or Tier Two interventions (O'Connor, 2003; Vaughn, 2003; Vaughn, Linan-Thompson, & Hickman, 2003; Vellutino et al., 1996). In most studies, 20%–25% of all students are exposed to a Tier One intervention. Further, 50%–66% of those lower functioning students exposed to Tier One interventions demonstrate sufficient growth such that they do not need to move on to Tier Two interventions. Finally, in Tier Two interventions, an additional 15%–25% make progress and do not move to Tier Three interventions (Fuchs & Fuchs, 2005; Marston, 2005). Thus, perhaps 25% of the students struggling in reading who are exposed to Tier One interventions may demonstrate a learning disability under RTI. Thus, 5%–6% of all students would seem to qualify for services as LD (calculated as 25% of the initial 25% of the population who demonstrate reading problems).

Although that calculation and the resulting estimate is very rough, it does give some indication that the percentage of students placed using RTI will not significantly decrease from the current levels of students identified as learning disabled.

EXAMPLE TWO: READING FLUENCY IN GRADE 3

Another example involving reading skill at a higher level may be in order. In this example, Perla, a third-grade student at Statham Elementary in Billings, Montana, is struggling with reading fluency. Although she seems generally adept at decoding words and her teacher, Ms. Drewry, has noted no specific phonological deficits to speak of, her fluency is below that of other children in Grade 3. As one may imagine, her reading fluency affects her reading comprehension skills; on the state testing program, Perla was in the lowest 20% of the students in the school on both reading fluency and reading comprehension at Grade 3. Ms. Drewry and the other teachers in her school used the *Open Court Reading Series*, which is a scientifically validated direct instructional program. At a minimum, a scientifically validated instructional curriculum has been implemented with Perla for the first three years of school.

Tier One Intervention

In applying the guidelines for Tier One intervention presented in Table 2.1, Ms. Drewry discusses Perla's reading challenges with the reading specialist, Dr. Drako. Dr. Drako recommends, as a Tier One intervention, that Ms. Drewry continue use of the *Open Court Reading Series* and follow Perla's progress a bit more closely. Thus, instruction will continue using the *Open Court* curriculum for the next grading period of six weeks, but a curriculum-based assessment on reading fluency will be implemented to monitor Perla's progress. Dr. Drako recommends monitoring twice each week, and assists Ms. Drewry with some suggestions on how to do that.

On Tuesday and Friday of each week, Ms. Drewry holds a five-minute reading session with Perla and presents a third-grade reading selection. As Perla orally reads, Ms. Drewry follows along on the same passage, marking the errors Perla makes. After a two-minute reading session, a count of "words read correctly" is taken and that count is divided by two to get a figure of "words read correctly per minute." Ms. Drewry then discusses each word Perla missed in that first reading, and then Perla repeats the reading a second time for two minutes. Again the count of words read correctly per minute is taken; that raw score is placed on a chart indicating Perla's oral reading fluency for that day. Thus, Perla's progress is monitored quite closely during her instruction using the *Open Court* reading series.

Dr. Drako, meanwhile, makes a point to observe Perla in a class-wide reading lesson from Open Court, as well as during one or two of the curriculum-based measurements completed by Ms. Drewry. Thus, Dr. Drako can address both Perla's response to intervention and Ms. Drewry's instruction procedures during the *Open Court* lessons. Within a six-week period, twelve data points are obtained on Perla's reading fluency. These data are presented in Figure 2.4.

Tier Two Intervention

As these data indicate, Perla made very little progress during this Tier One intervention and only averaged about thirty words read correctly per minute, a low reading fluency rate for Grade 3. These data seem to suggest

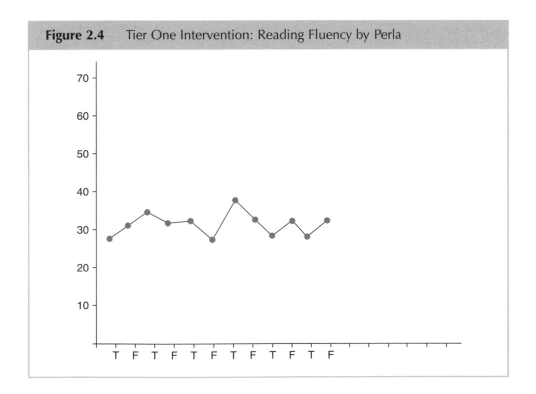

Figure 2.4　Tier One Intervention: Reading Fluency by Perla

that Perla requires a more intensive intervention than merely participation in *Open Court* with the class and brief repeated readings with Ms. Drewry. After that six-week period, Ms. Drewry consults with Dr. Drako and determines that Perla has not responded well to the Tier One intervention, and a Tier Two intervention must be considered.

At this point, both Dr. Drako and Ms. Drewry discuss various scientifically validated curriculum that would be appropriate to address the specific reading challenge demonstrated by Perla—reading fluency. In this case, Dr. Drako, as a reading specialist, can provide more specific knowledge of various reading curricula. Dr. Drako recommends the *Read Naturally* curriculum, which was recently published by Read Naturally, Inc., of Saint Paul, Minnesota (2006). That curriculum has been scientifically validated and has been utilized for RTI determinations.

Reflection 2.3	What Is the Best Variable to Assess During RTI?

What type of reading measures should be utilized for RTI? In the example, Perla has a documented reading fluency deficit. As the example unfolds, fluency is the major measure assessed. However, reading includes a wide variety of variables, and in many cases it may not be clear which specific measure or measures should be utilized for the student's progress monitoring. For example, although Perla has been described as manifesting a deficit in reading fluency but not in decoding, it is possible for a student to have a phonological deficit, which affects both fluency and decoding. In that instance, a measure of the child's phonemic or phonics skills would be a more appropriate variable to measure during the RTI process. The variable assessed during the RTI should be the variable most closely linked to the student's actual or suspected deficit and most closely tied to actual reading achievement.

Reflection 2.4	How Do I Find and Select Scientifically Validated Curricula for RTI?

Although educators have long held the belief that instructional methods and curricula should be supported by rigorous scientific studies, the No Child Left Behind legislation represents the first time that the federal government has mandated scientific support for the reading instructional curricula utilized. In short, teachers are now expected to understand the scientific validity studies that support the curricula utilized. This begs the question: How can a teacher find and select appropriate, scientifically validated curricula for specific reading problems? Of course, teachers—like all professionals—should routinely read scientific journals in their respective fields such as the *Reading Research Quarterly,* the *Elementary School Journal*, the *Journal of Learning Disabilities,* and many others. These journals often publish validation studies for new curricula. Also, general education teachers should frequently consult with reading specialists, special educators, school psychologists, and/or curriculum specialists about individual students' specific problems.

Next, several Web sites are available that specifically present information on scientifically validated curriculum (Otaiba & Rivera, 2006).

http://www.fcrr.org. The Florida Center for Reading Research disseminates information on a wide variety of reading curricula, ranging from preschool to Grade 12. Initially this site included documentation of the research basis, but that has been temporarily removed and the procedures are undergoing review. Look under FCRR Reports for analyses of the available reading curricula.

http://reading.uoregon.edu/curricula/or_rfc_review_2.php. This site provides summaries for various reading programs and a synopsis of the research behind them. The site emphasizes large reading curricula that are intended for use as either whole class curricula or in small-group instruction. This site also provides information on many supplemental reading programs that would be appropriate for either Tier Two or Tier Three interventions.

http://www.nctm.org. This site for the National Council of Teachers of Mathematics presents information on research-based mathematics curricula, as well as the national standards for mathematics.

http://www.k8accesscenter.org. The Access Center is a national technical assistance center funded by the U.S. Department of Education's Office of Special Education Programs. The site contains a research continuum that outlines criteria for evaluation of research-based strategies, along with an evaluation of several strategies.

http://www.w-w-c.org. The What Works Clearinghouse was established in 2002 by the U.S. Department of Education's Institute of Education Sciences to provide educators, policymakers, researchers, and the public with a central and trusted source of scientific evidence of what works in education. This site reviews research studies in several areas; evaluation of math curricula are currently available. Reading interventions are currently under review and are not yet available here, but scientific evaluations of research on reading curricula should be available from this site by 2007.

Finally, while not providing an exhaustive list, we wanted to present some of the more commonly used curricula that have received scientific validation via a number of different research studies. These are listed in Appendix C. With these various resources at hand, teachers can find scientifically validated curricula for Tier One, Tier Two, and Tier Three interventions.

Perla participated in the computerized version of the *Read Naturally* curriculum for the next grading period. This generated scores on both reading fluency and reading comprehension each day for the following three weeks, as presented in Figure 2.5. By using the computerized version of this curriculum, Perla was able to complete her reading class work each day without the teacher having to sit and read each reading selection along with Perla. This is one example of an intensive Tier Two intervention that does not require immediate and total teacher attention.

As these data demonstrate, this intensive intervention was quite successful for Perla. During this six-week period, Perla's reading fluency increased from an average of thirty words per minute to an average of approximately forty-five words per minute. Her reading comprehension increased from three to five questions correct to nine or ten questions correct. Perla did require a more intensive reading intervention than that offered by the *Open Court* reading curriculum presented to her classmates. Her progress on an intensive Tier Two intervention, however, demonstrated that Perla can and did respond quite favorably to an intervention that was directly targeted towards her specific reading problem. Thus, it should be concluded that Perla did not manifest a learning disability; rather, she needed an intervention and reading program that addressed her reading deficits more directly than the *Open Court* series.

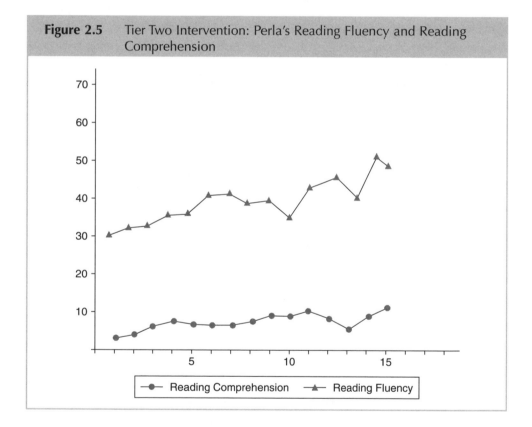

Figure 2.5 Tier Two Intervention: Perla's Reading Fluency and Reading Comprehension

THE STANDARD PROTOCOL RTI PACKAGE

In the examples of the performance of Caleb and Perla, certain common elements were documented during the RTI process. Taken together, these elements demonstrated the various deficits noted among these two students, while protecting these students' rights for free appropriate public education in the least restrictive environment. The second example is an illustration of an instructional deficit remediated without mislabeling a child as learning disabled. Protection of these children's rights is a critical concern; that is the main reason for having an RTI process. Thus, for all RTIs, the following elements for the standard protocol RTI package are recommended:

1. A screening score indicating a potential problem;

2. A Tier One intervention data set indicating nonresponse or less than adequate response to Tier One intervention;

3. Observational notes indicating that the general education teacher implemented a scientifically based curriculum in Tier One with fidelity;

4. A Tier Two intervention data set indicating nonresponse or less than adequate response to a Tier Two intensive educational intervention;

5. Observational data indicating that an intensive research-based intervention was undertaken for the Tier Two intervention; and

6. A summary report of these basic elements and recommendations for further services for learning disabilities, if warranted by these data. After the Tier Two intervention is completed, a summary report should be completed, regardless of the eligibility determination.

These are not the only elements that must be included. At a minimum, documentation of appropriate parental notifications should be included at various points in the process. Further, documentation of consultations between educators should be noted, and certainly such consultation should be mandatory prior to the initiation of Tier Two interventions. However, documentation of the six aforementioned elements is critical to both implement the RTI procedure correctly and protect the rights of the child to not be mislabeled with a disability. Although these elements may be documented in a variety of ways, an "RTI Summary and Observation Form" is presented in Appendix D which may be used to document these specific elements.

The data that should be included in the various sections on this form are the following:

A Step-by-Step Guide for Educators. One strength of this approach is the involvement with a second teacher in this observational phase in the early steps of the process. In this model, we recommend that, prior to moving into Tier Two interventions, some consultation on the child's problem be considered mandatory. Thus, at a minimum, the teacher and the person doing the observation should meet to discuss the results of the Tier One intervention.

Alternatively, for students who continue to demonstrate problems, a meeting should be held involving the general education teacher, the independent observer, the child's parents and perhaps other personnel involved with the child's education, and persons who may have particular expertise in areas where the child needs more intensive instruction. The notes at this step should summarize the discussion from that consultation meeting as well as note decisions concerning which curriculum to implement in Tier Two of this RTI. The steps are:

Tier Two Intervention and Intervention Summary. This section should present a description of the Tier Two intervention implemented with the child. The summary should note the duration of that intervention and the manner in which the teacher monitored pupil progress. A chart of the student's performance data over time should be attached.

Observation of Instruction and Tier Two Intervention. Another educator with appropriate expertise should observe this child during instruction at some point during the Tier Two intervention. That observer should have relevant expertise in either the academic area in which the instruction takes place or in special education practices. Notes should include a brief summary of observations conducted by other educators during either the initial instruction or the Tier One intervention. Like the Tier One observation summary, it should include comments as to the appropriateness and scientific validation of the curricula utilized as well as the instructional applications of the curricula. Finally, this observation should note any relevant student responses to the instruction that may be important for discussion.

Summary Report. At this point, if the child is not making acceptable progress, the team should meet once again and complete an eligibility evaluation for this student. Thus, special education legislative mandates such as notification of parents, consideration of alternative placements, and so on begin at this point. However, school district personnel should not wait until this point to actively involve parents in this RTI process. Indeed, we encourage parental involvement from the outset and encourage general education teachers to talk with parents about academic problems during the Tier One intervention phase. Certainly by the time of the summary report, parent notification should be documented. Participation of all parties to include all teachers, consultants, and observers for this child is mandatory. The summary report will then note the collective decisions and recommendations made by the group. Figure 2.6 presents such a report on Caleb, the first student described in this chapter. When coupled with the two data charts (presented in Figures 2.3 and 2.4), these data

Table 2.3   Guidelines for Streamlining the Standard Treatment Protocol

1. Make certain that the reading curriculum utilized in the general education classrooms is a research-validated instructional curriculum and that teachers are trained in the use of that curriculum. If those conditions are met, then the "Tier One" intervention may become merely a "progress monitoring" of the child's progress on a weekly basis, and not a separate instructional intervention that must be implemented.

2. Train faculty in interventions that have a sound scientific base, in order to ensure treatment fidelity. In that sense, implementation of RTI can benefit all students, not only students who might be eligible for special services.

3. Use content experts as the independent observers for Tier One and Tier Two. In the case of a reading disability, use a reading teacher, a master-level general education/special education teacher, or a school psychologist with expertise in instruction for those observations.

4. Using persons who would be spending time assessing the child under the traditional discrepancy-based paradigm (i.e., a school psychologist), as the observer offers the option of replacing one set of eligibility duties of that person with another. Thus, no additional resources are needed and fewer resources will be required because the eligibility determination no longer requires such extensive individualized assessment.

5. Use a different observer for the Tier One and Tier Two interventions when possible. In that fashion, more educators have actually seen how the student responds to intervention, and thus more will be qualified to suggest additional instructional ideas.

6. For Tier Two interventions, develop systems whereby students who need a Tier Two intervention may join in small-group instruction that is already ongoing in the school. For example, many Title One programs and/or various early intervention programs in reading or math involve small-group instruction (as is required in Tier Two). Thus, for Tier Two interventions, students may be assigned to those groups for one grading period, and their progress may be charted either daily or weekly.

7. Prior to Tier Three interventions, an eligibility committee must meet and formally determine that the child has not been responsive to instruction in Tier One and Tier Two. Thus, a committee meeting is called for whenever a student is unresponsive in Tier Two. After that committee meets, the child is identified as a student with a learning disability and the Tier Three intervention takes place under the rubric of special educational services.

constitute a completed RTI. Most standard treatment protocol RTIs will be similar to this.

A Streamlined Standard Treatment Protocol Process

Given the aforementioned requirements, some educators may wonder what might be done to streamline this process while still generating the

Figure 2.6a An RTI Summary Form

An RTI Summary Form

Pupil **Caleb Tooks**   Date **10/25/06**

Initiating Teacher's Name **Janice Westall**

School Address **Beaverdam Elementary**

Pupil's Grade **2**   Pupil's Homeroom Teacher **Janice Westall**

Teacher's Statement of Academic Problem:

I noticed Caleb had extreme difficulty reading independently. This difficulty was noticed on CRCT (Criterion Referred Critical Skills Test) where his score in April of last year was only at the kindergarten level. The scaled score was 83 showing a reading deficit in vocabulary in April of last year.

~J. Westall

Description of Tier One Intervention:

In the second grade, Caleb had been using the open count reading series, which is a scientifically validated reading program. I charted his mastery of new words once a week for the first 8 weeks of school (see chart A attached) and he is learning only an average of 1 new vocabulary term per week.

~J. Westall

Observation of General Instruction and Tier One Intervention.

AS PRINCIPAL, I OBSERVED MS. WESTALL IN HER READING INSTRUCTION ON 9/18/06, NOTING PARTICULARLY THAT SHE FOLLOWED THE LESSON PLAN IN THE TEACHER MANUAL THAT DAY. SHE CALLED ON CALEB TOOKS TWICE DURING THOSE VOCABULARY PRACTICE ACTIVITIES AND CALEB ANSWERED THE FIRST QUESTION CORRECTLY. HE DID NOT RESPOND TO THE SECOND.

-MS. TAMMY WILEY
PRINCIPAL

Figure 2.6b

Tier One Intervention Summary:

As shown in chart 2.2, Caleb can only recognize a very limited number of words. He seems to try to sound out various terms but still is not increasing his vocabulary recognition, often missing even the initial consonant sounds.

~J. Westall

Post Tier One Meeting Notes:

Ms. Westall, Ms. Wiley, and I met to discuss an intensive intervention in reading for Caleb Tooks on 9/30/06. As a reading teacher, I can work with Caleb in the Direct Instruction SRA reading program for 20 minutes each day at 8:30am, Caleb will join a reading group of 4 other students and I will chart his word recognition skills each day.

~Ms. Renee Jones

Observation of Instruction and Tier Two Intervention.

I OBSERVED MS. JONES WORK WITH CALEB AND SEVERAL OTHER STUDENTS ON 10/22/06, IN USING THE SRA READING MATERIALS, CALEB PARTICIPATED IN THE SESSIONS AND RESPONDED CORRECTLY EACH TIME HE WAS CALLED UPON. MS. JONES WAS OPTIMISTIC ABOUT HIS PROGRESS.

-MS. WILEY

Tier Two Intervention Summary:

THE DAILY DATE IN CHART 2.2 INDICATED THAT THIS INTERVENTION IS NOT WORKING FOR CALEB, AT THIS POINT, FURTHER INDIVIDUAL INTERVENTIONS ARE REQUIRED. THE TEAM RECOMMENDS PLACEMENT OF CALEB INTO THE SPECIAL EDUCATION PROGRAM FOR LEARNING DISABILITIES, WITH HIS PRIMARY SERVICE IN MS. WESTALL'S CLASS AND ONE PERIOD PER DAY IN THE RESEARCH ROOM FOR INDIVIDUAL TEACHING INSTRUCTION.

-MS. WILEY

information required to document RTI progress and protect the child's rights to a fair and impartial consideration as to his or her eligibility. With that in mind, Table 2.3 presents guidelines that might be implemented to streamline this process. Also, Appendix E presents some additional suggestions concerning how teachers might find additional time to facilitate the RTI process.

CONCLUSION

Moving into implementation of the standard treatment protocol RTI will not be easy, as many teachers are not presently conducting pupil progress monitoring at this level of specificity. Further, there are many unanswered questions concerning RTI (addressed in a later chapter); these must be addressed during the implementation of RTI. Many researchers recommend further professional development for teachers as our nation begins to utilize these procedures (Fuchs & Fuchs, 2005; Gersten & Dimino, 2006; Mellard et. al. 2004).

However, there are many additional factors that will facilitate increased implementation of RTI. For these reasons, the standard treatment protocol may be more easily implemented than other RTI models. First, as noted previously, many curricula are presently structured to allow for pupil progress monitoring on a daily or biweekly basis, and implementation of these curricula should be fairly simple for the veteran teachers. Next, the emphasis on curriculum-based measurement over the last two decades will make this type of instruction somewhat more understandable. Finally, once shown the procedures, teachers should find that these instructional techniques effectively enhance their instructional competence in many ways for many of their students. Thus, from a teacher's perspective, RTI will tend to become a self-reinforcing process.

REFERENCES

Deno, S. L. (2003). Development in curriculum-based measurement. *Journal of Special Education, 37*(3), 184–192.

Fuchs, D., & Fuchs, L. S. (2005). Responsiveness-to-intervention: A blueprint for practitioners, policymakers, and parents. *TEACHING Exceptional Children, 38*(1), 57–61.

Fuchs, D., & Fuchs, L. S. (2006). Introduction to Response to intervention : What, why, and how valid is it? *Reading Research Quarterly, 41*(1), 93–98.

Fuchs, D., Fuchs, L. S., & Compton, D. L. (2004). Identifying reading disabilities by responsiveness-to-instruction: Specifying measures and criteria. *Learning Disability Quarterly, 27*, 216–227.

Gersten, R., & Dimino, J. A. (2006). RTI (Response to Intervention): Rethinking special education for students with reading difficulties (yet again). *Reading Research Quarterly, 41*(1), 99–108.

Marston, D. (2005). Tiers of intervention in responsiveness to intervention: Prevention outcomes and learning disabilities patterns. *Journal of Learning Disabilities, 38* (6), 529–546.

Marston, D., Muyskens, P., Lau, M., & Canter, A. (2003). Problem solving model for decision-making with high-incidence disabilities: The Minneapolis experience. *Learning Disabilities Research & Practice, 18*(3), 187–200.

Mastropieri, M. A., & Scruggs, T. W. (2005). Feasibility and consequences of Response to Intervention: Examination of the issues and scientific evidence as a model for the identification of individuals with learning disabilities, *Journal of Learning Disabilities, 38*(6), 525–531.

Mellard, D. F., Byrd, S. E., Johnson, E., Tollefson, J. M., & Boesche, L. (2004). Foundations and research on identifying model responsiveness-to-intervention sites. *Learning Disability Quarterly, 27,* 243–255.

National Joint Committee on Learning Disabilities. (2005). Responsiveness to intervention and learning disabilities: A report prepared by the National Joint Committee on Learning Disabilities. *Learning Disability Quarterly 28*(4), 249–260.

O'Connor, R. (2003, December). *Tiers of intervention in kindergarten through third grade.* Paper presented at the National Research Center on Learning Disabilities responsiveness-to-intervention symposium, Kansas City, MO. (See the discussion of this paper in Marston et al., 2003.)

Otaiba, S. A., & Rivera, M. O. (2006). Individualizing guided oral reading fluency instruction for students with emotional and behavioral disorders. *Intervention in School and Clinic, 41*(3), 144–149.

Read Naturally, Inc. (2006). *Read naturally masters edition.* Saint Paul, MN: Author.

Vaughn, S. (2003, December). *How many tiers are needed for Response to Intervention to achieve acceptable prevention out-comes.* Presented at the National Research Center on Learning Disabilities Responsiveness-to-Intervention Symposium, Kansas City, MO.

Vaughn, S., Linan-Thompson, S., & Hickman, P. (2003). Response to treatment as a means of identifying students with reading/learning disabilities. *Exceptional Children, 69*(4), 391–409.

Vellutino, F. R., Scanlon, D. M., Sipay, E. R., Small, S., Chen, R., Pratt, A., et al. (1996). Cognitive profiles of difficult to remediate and readily remediated poor readers: Early intervention as a vehicle for distinguishing between cognition and experiential deficits as basic cause of specific reading disability. *Journal of Educational Psychology, 88,* 601–638.

3 Implementation of a Problem-Solving Response to Intervention

Cara Shores and William N. Bender

The problem-solving model for Response to Intervention, as described in Chapter 1, has many similarities to the standard treatment protocol model, which was described in the previous chapter. In both the problem-solving model and the standard treatment protocol, for example, interventions are usually implemented in three or four tiers and become more intensive with each tier. Progression to the next tier is recommended if a student shows inadequate response to the current intervention. There are, however, some very distinct differences between these two models, as we will point out in this discussion of the problem-solving model. In particular, these differences lie primarily in the decision-making process and the types of interventions provided.

The structure of the problem-solving RTI is often less formal than that of the standard treatment protocol, simply due to the fact that it requires flexibility in options for interventions and resources. However, this does not mean that the problem-solving model is unstructured. In fact, the problem-solving model must have a defined structure in order to keep it from becoming haphazard in implementation. Agencies contemplating implementation of the problem-solving model should give careful consideration to the issues and suggestions presented in this chapter.

Problem-solving RTIs were first used in behavioral consultation (Fuchs, Mock, Morgan, & Young, 2003). The process may be described as inductive, empirical, and behavioral, with the key element being that it is inductive. Proponents of this model argue that no one intervention fits all students; interventions are effective only when the team takes the individual learning needs of the student into account. In problem-solving RTI models, team members meet to discuss individual student needs and develop interventions based on those needs. Although there may be more than one student involved in the implementation of the intervention, the strategy is designed specifically to address the individual student's problem. Teams then evaluate the outcome of the intervention and adjust the instructional strategy based on the student-achievement data.

In general, the problem-solving RTI is typically the model preferred by educators and practitioners. However, this model has received criticism from researchers. These criticisms usually stem from the lack of empirical research and valid data concerning the implementation and outcomes of the problem-solving RTI model. In the few instances in which research has been completed, the studies have "failed to produce persuasive evidence that classroom-based interventions are implemented with fidelity, strengthen students' academic achievement, or improve classroom behavior" (Fuchs et al., 2003, p. 163).

In any RTI, teachers should implement the research-proven curricula or strategies with instructional rigor and precision. Still, with that stated, we recognize that most interventions in RTI will be carried out by classroom teachers—or in some cases, teaching assistants—in the public school classroom. Such settings present demands that often interrupt the educational process. Certainly, the majority of schools do not have researchers, graduate assistants, or even full-time support teachers who can carry out all interventions. Also, some educational interventions may be characterized by frequent interruptions (since interruptions frequently occur in schools); thus, the lessons may end prior to completion. Most interventions can, however, be properly implemented by teachers or teacher assistants who have been trained in the technique. For training and follow-up, we have suggested observation by administrators or others trained in the technique. We believe that such observations must occur in order to document that these research-based strategies are implemented with fidelity and, thus, are effective.

Decisions from RTI involve eligibility placements for children, and thus affect their lives in significant ways. Therefore, decisions made in the problem-solving model, like decisions made in the standard treatment protocol, must be data-based decisions. Teams should choose interventions that are research based and validated, and data derived from frequent progress monitoring should drive decision making and instruction. Teachers must use curriculum-based measurement to monitor how well all their students are doing, and step up the frequency of curriculum-based measurement for the students receiving interventions.

Reflection 3.1	What Research-Based Strategies Do I Have in My Teaching Repertoire?

As teachers seek to implement research-based strategies in the classroom, they often find that their knowledge of these research-based instructional strategies is quite limited. This is due to the fact that teachers have not previously been expected to document the research basis for the instructional curricula they implemented. As an example, you may wish to make a list of research-based strategies that you currently use in your classroom, for which you are sure there is scientific validation research available. Although most teachers can list several such curricula, few teachers are well acquainted with the range of curricula that are available. The Web sites listed in Reflection 2.4 in Chapter 2 contain various resources on the most commonly used research-based interventions in various skill areas.

In Chapter 1, we presented two well-known models of problem-solving RTI: the Heartland Area Educational Agency model and the Minneapolis Public Schools model. Some problems with these particular models have been pointed out by researchers. Perhaps the most significant of these issues is appropriateness of interventions and treatment fidelity. For example, Flugum and Reschly (1994) studied the quality of pre-referral interventions in Heartland Area Educational Agency's schools. According to their study, teams were providing few interventions and the ones provided were of poor quality. In a similar study, Marston (as reported in Fuchs et al., 2003) looked at the quality of interventions in the Minneapolis Public Schools model and reported that they were "of superior quality." However, Fuchs et al. (2003) point out that "superior" is not explained or defined, and this raises questions concerning the quality of the interventions received. Further, Fuchs et al. (2003) raise questions concerning the accuracy and extent of the data on student progress over time in that study.

In a review of the Minneapolis Public Schools Guidelines for Problem-Solving Model Implementation, we were unable to find requirements for research-based interventions. It states that the model "emphasizes the use of multiple intervention strategies" (Minneapolis Public Schools, 2002, p. 1), but does not state that the interventions must have a research base. In another of their documents (Minneapolis Public Schools, 2006, p. 2), it is stated that the team will develop "alternative interventions, which may include: re-mediation from building specialists or educational assistants,

Title I support, help from Limited English Proficiency staff, and/or consultation from special education staff." There was no documentation of the specific methods or interventions that might be implemented. This follows the idea that the problem-solving model is inductive and based on student need. It may, however, leave too much flexibility—which could result in poor-quality strategies being implemented and/or poor monitoring of student progress. Both of these factors will negatively impact the overall quality of the RTI process.

In this chapter, we will present several examples of how problem-solving RTIs might be implemented. We will discuss the issues raised here and provide guidance on ways that systems might address these concerns.

THE PROBLEM-SOLVING RTI PACKAGE

As a result of No Child Left Behind, most schools currently administer benchmark testing as part of the educational procedures for all students. This data can be used by teachers to identify which students are not making progress and are in need of additional instructional interventions (Grimes & Kurns, 2003). One strength of RTI is that implementation of either model will have the effect of causing teachers to critically evaluate the impact of their instruction for all students who are struggling in school. It is essential to monitor student progress at this level to quickly identify students who are not progressing as they should. When particular students are identified as needing assistance, implementation of the RTI process should begin.

As is the case for standard treatment protocol, the problem-solving RTI is most often divided into three or four tiers. In our three-tiered model, Tier One involves implementation of a scientifically validated curriculum or strategy in the general education classroom for the child who is experiencing difficulty. As discussed in Chapter 2, this may involve the same instruction that is presented to the rest of the students in the class at a more intensive level, or it may involve a separate intervention. In either case, it is recommended that progress monitoring occur on a weekly or biweekly basis for students receiving interventions in Tier One. Students who do not show adequate progress are given more intensive instruction or interventions at Tier Two. Curriculum-based assessment continues on a weekly or more frequent basis and growth is charted to give a visual representation of student progress. Students who, again, do not show adequate progress are moved to Tier Three for possible further assessment and/or consideration for IDEA eligibility and special education services.

It is important to note here that there are several different versions of tiered models of intervention. For example, the University of Texas's

Center for Reading and Language Arts advocates a three-tiered model in which Tier One involves all children in the general curriculum, Tier Two involves supplemental instruction for children not successful in Tier One, and Tier Three involves additional supplemental instruction for children not successful in Tier Two. In their model, special education consideration occurs after Tier Three and is separate from the tier pyramid (Hall, 2006, p. 12). Other agencies have adopted a combined model in which Tier One includes all children on the general curriculum, Tiers Two and Three involve intensive interventions and progress monitoring, and Tier Four involves consideration for IDEA eligibility (Tilley, 2003). Each school system should evaluate its structure and resources to determine which model is most appropriate. However, regardless of which tiered structure is chosen, the guiding principles and concepts remain the same.

In problem-solving RTIs, a team approach is used from the outset of the process. The standard treatment protocol, as described in Chapter 2, does not require a team approach until well into the process. At the school level, the membership of the Problem-Solving Team may be constant—this is called the Core Teams Approach—or flexible (Flex Teams Approach), depending on the needs and resources specific to the school. Core teams are those whose basic membership holds expertise in relevant instructional areas, and the team members remain the same. Often these teams are composed of math coaches, literacy coaches, school psychologists, curriculum coordinators, or behavior specialists. Other team members may come from outside agencies, as is the case with Heartland Area Educational Agency. Other individuals, such as school nurses or special education teachers, may be brought in to consult with the team as needed for particular students.

Flex teams are made up of teachers from the student's grade level, as well as other education professionals mentioned in the previous paragraph. Its membership is more flexible because it varies based on the student's grade level or on curricular or behavioral needs.

The basis for most versions of the problem-solving RTI model is a cyclical problem-solving process involving four steps (Deno, 2002; Grimes & Kurns, 2003). In each tier, a problem-solving team addresses the four steps and determines the best course of action for the student. In order to distinguish this cyclical problem-solving process from the problem-solving model of RTI, we have named the cycle "DPIE," relating to the four steps of the cycle:

D Define the Problem

P Plan an Intervention

I Implement the Intervention

E Evaluate the Student's Progress

Figure 3.1   The Problem-Solving Cycle

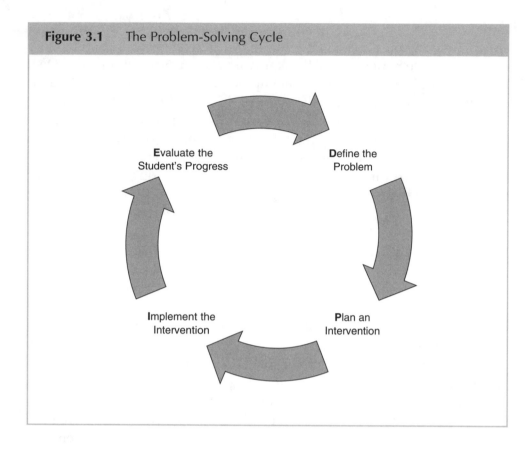

Define the Problem

As illustrated in Figure 3.1, Step 1 of the process begins with the definition and analysis of the student's problem. It is extremely important at this point to attempt to determine the cause of the student's difficulty and to define the problem completely and in objective, measurable terms. All relevant data and information regarding the child's functioning should be examined.

In many instances, it may be appropriate to collect information about the student's functioning outside of the classroom (Grimes & Kurns, 2003; Marston, Muyskens, Lau, & Canter, 2003). We believe this is important for several reasons. First, children come to school with a variety of backgrounds and experiences; common sense tells us they don't leave those experiences at the classroom door. In fact, these outside-of-school experiences often determine how well the student performs in school (Maslow & Lowery, 1998). Basic needs must be met before we can move on to more abstract activities such as learning. When children are hungry, sleepy, or fear for their safety, academics may seem irrelevant to their lives. Today's students live in a difficult world. The issues they face affect every aspect of life. School is the institution in which children spend approximately one-third of each day, ten months of the year, of their childhood and adolescence. If we are to address the problems that occur in the classroom, we often must learn as much as we can about the students' lives outside of the classroom.

Second, if a student moves through all tiers and is eventually considered for IDEA eligibility, information must come from a variety of data-based sources, such as parent input, teacher recommendations, information about the child's physical condition, social or cultural background, and/or adaptive behavior assessments. It is most helpful to have this information at the beginning of the process to aid the team in determining appropriate resources and interventions for the student.

Any relevant sources of information on a student should be fully explored. Background information forms completed by parents can yield a wealth of knowledge. Team members should carefully review the information for clues that would point to the student's current problems. Information such as delayed development, health issues, or disruptions to normal development obtained in an initial background form may signal a need for follow-up investigation.

Although using RTI procedures to determine eligibility for LD services is the focus of this text, the RTI process also may be used to address behavioral problems. It is recommended in these instances that teachers complete a functional behavioral analysis to gather data to be used in this and subsequent phases of the process. The analysis should include information such as setting, frequency, time and duration of behavior problems, the activity occurring at the time of the behavior problem, and the student's response to imposed or natural consequences. Data should be analyzed to identify patterns of behavior in order to determine the cause of the behavior and appropriate strategies for intervention.

Plan an Intervention

The next step of the problem-solving process, Step 2, is to set a goal and develop an intervention plan containing one or more strategies or interventions designed to specifically address the student's problem. The goal for the student should be based on their baseline data and a projection of appropriate growth based on expected progress for the grade level (e.g., benchmark data). Based on IDEA requirements, it is clear that the strategies should be scientific, research-based interventions specific to the child's particular need. Again, both selection of a scientifically proven curriculum and treatment fidelity for instruction in that curriculum are critical. The team must select the right intervention and ensure that appropriate instruction is provided.

Next, the team must determine the timeline for plan implementation. Recommendations regarding timelines on these interventions range from six to twelve weeks (Fuchs, Fuchs, McMaster, Yen, & Svenson, 2004; Hall, 2006) and will depend on the specific intervention selected, the severity of the student's problem, and/or other factors as determined by the team. It may be appropriate, for example, to plan interventions that coincide with a single six- or nine-week grading period, whereas in other cases a shorter intervention may be appropriate. Such decisions are left to the school-based team. The team must also decide when and how progress will be monitored. It is helpful to specify who is responsible for implementation and progress monitoring (Grimes & Kurns, 2003).

Implement the Intervention

Step 3 involves implementation of the plan. The interventions must be carried out with accuracy and fidelity. Observations from administrators should verify that the intervention is being implemented as it was intended. Daily, weekly, or biweekly progress monitoring should be utilized to document positive or negative response to the intervention. Teachers may use any relevant form of curriculum-based assessment to measure student progress.

Evaluate the Student's Progress

Step 4 of the process involves a team meeting. After a sufficient time for the intervention, the team should meet and discuss whether the intervention is working for the student. All relevant data showing progress over time should be used to reevaluate the student's functioning and determine the next steps for the student. These data should include some time-sensitive information, such as data charts that measure a child's progress daily or weekly, and may include other data such as class grades or group-administered assessments. Based on these data, the team may decide to continue the current strategy, implement a new strategy, move to the next tier, or take the student back to instruction in the general curriculum with other students. Again, we want to stress the point that all decisions should be data driven. Team members cannot make informed decisions without sufficient data; the more data points available to the team, the better equipped the members will be in determining what should occur next.

This problem-solving cycle is essentially repeated for each intervention, and through each tier. This makes the problem-solving model of RTI highly responsive to the needs of the students. With each intervention, the instruction should become more complex and more intensive as students move through the instruction and thus master the targeted skills. Also, as they move into Tiers Two and Three, the problem-solving process, by virtue of becoming more specific and intense, may well require more resources to address the student's needs. School personnel should anticipate that need and plan accordingly (Grimes & Kurns, 2003).

Reflection 3.2	Is Training Needed for Implementation of the Problem-Solving Process (DPIE)?

The problem-solving cycle is designed to apply the scientific method to the problem-solving process. Although many teachers may be familiar with this process, not all teachers will be. Thus, practitioners should consider the need for training in this tactic. Here are some reflective questions that may guide you in your consideration of the training that may be necessary. First, is the problem-solving cycle being used by any other teams at your school? Next, do additional teachers need to be trained in the process? If so, what resources are available for your school to access training of this kind?

An important consideration for teams in both the problem-solving and the standard protocol RTI is how to determine sufficient progress. We recommend the use of a "dual discrepancy" focus on performance level and growth (Fuchs, 2003; Speece, Case, & Molloy, 2003). In the dual discrepancy focus, the two types of data to consider involve (1) a comparison between the student and his or her peers and (2) the student's growth from the beginning to the end of the intervention, also known as "slope." It is important to consider both types of information in order to get a complete picture of the student's responsiveness to intervention. If the team considers how the student compares to peers after intervention and finds that the student still falls in the lowest 20%, it is unclear whether the student benefited from the intervention, even if he or she did demonstrate academic growth on his or her individual charted data. The team must also consider the growth, or slope, of the student's progress, comparing data points before, during, and after the intervention. A student who makes significant gains but is still below his or her peers may need continued intervention using the same type of strategies, perhaps at a more complex level. A student who begins at a level that is 20% below his or her peers but makes very little progress may need to proceed to the next intervention tier. Viewing the two pieces of information together gives the more accurate and complete picture of student responsiveness. This information is easily interpreted when visually represented through charting. Figure 3.2 presents a data chart showing these data.

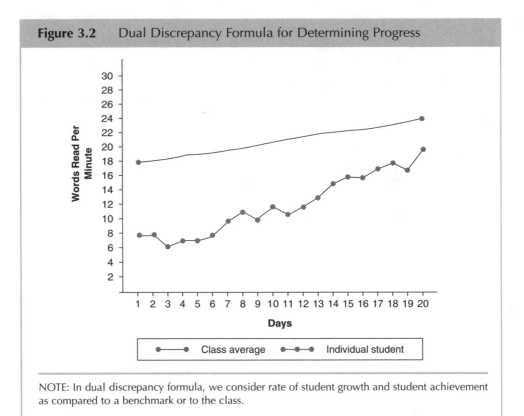

Figure 3.2   Dual Discrepancy Formula for Determining Progress

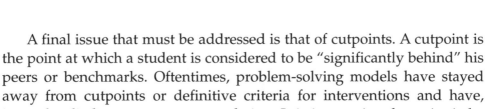

NOTE: In dual discrepancy formula, we consider rate of student growth and student achievement as compared to a benchmark or to the class.

A final issue that must be addressed is that of cutpoints. A cutpoint is the point at which a student is considered to be "significantly behind" his peers or benchmarks. Oftentimes, problem-solving models have stayed away from cutpoints or definitive criteria for interventions and have, instead, relied on team recommendation. It is imperative that criteria be established to define when interventions are needed. But at what point should that happen?

Some researchers have set a guideline cutpoint as one standard deviation below the achievement of the class; others have suggested the lowest 25% achievement level as a cutpoint (Fuchs, 2003). In much of the RTI literature, the second and third tiers involve the lowest 10%–20% achievement level of the class (Colorado Department of Education Exceptional Student Services Unit, 2005). Although ongoing research is needed to clarify appropriate cutpoints for academic achievement, in both level and slope (Speece et al., 2003), for now we recommend that students in the lowest 20% of the class achievement level be considered in need of RTI interventions.

Table 3.1 lists guidelines for implementation of the problem-solving RTI. As you read through the next section of this chapter, which provides examples of this model, note the progression through the guidelines and

Table 3.1   Guidelines for Problem-Solving RTI

1. The teacher identifies students who are not making adequate progress in the general curriculum. The student must obtain an appropriate score on a general screening measure specific to the student's problem, or fall below the general academic ability in comparison with peers, as measured by a general screening measure. The teacher can easily gather this information with whole-class benchmark testing.

2. When the screening score indicates an academic score in the bottom 20%–25% of the population, the teacher initiates the Tier One cycle to develop an intervention plan.

3. The Problem-Solving Team meets together and implements the cycle, completing Steps 1 and 2 during the problem-solving meeting. The team should carefully document their decision-making process, including specific information about the research-based intervention to be implemented, procedures and tools for progress monitoring, persons responsible for both, and the timeline to be followed. The team should also make sure the teacher or person responsible for implementing the intervention is fully trained in its method.

4. The teacher or other personnel implement the intervention plan. During an intervention session, a school administrator, subject area specialist, literacy or math coach (whichever is appropriate), or other qualified person should observe the teacher and prepare a set of notes attesting to the implementation of the curriculum or strategy in a manner commensurate with the recommended teaching procedures.

5. Because Tier One interventions are a function of the general education classroom, these interventions are available to all students. Thus, implementation of Tier One interventions does not require specific notification of parents, although teachers would typically be expected to communicate with all parents regarding the general progress of their children.

6. Tier One interventions should result in a minimum of six data points or six assessments of progress, which allow the teacher to determine how the student responded to intervention a minimum of six times over a specified time period, which may be from six to twelve weeks. This should involve assessments at least once a week.

7. The Problem-Solving Team meets to review and evaluate student data. The team may decide to continue the strategy, try a different strategy, discontinue tiered interventions (if the student has made adequate progress), or move to a Tier Two intervention. If the team decides to continue with strategies in either Tier One or Two, the cycle begins again.

the DPIE. We will illustrate the problem-solving RTI model at elementary, middle, and high school levels of instruction in various curriculum areas.

EXAMPLE ONE: PHONEMIC AWARENESS: KINDERGARTEN

Lauren is a student in Ms. Kelly's kindergarten classroom. Lauren receives reading instruction in a group with six other children, using the *Rigby*

Literacy Reading Series. It is mid-November, and Ms. Kelly is concerned that Lauren is not able to consistently assign the correct sounds to letters. For example, when asked to name the first sound in the word "ball," Lauren is unable to identify the /b/ sound. When asked to identify the sounds that are the same in the words "like, look, and lake," Lauren often answers incorrectly. When reminded that it is the same sound as in her name, Lauren answers correctly.

Ms. Kelly administers the "Initial Sounds Fluency" subtest of the Diagnostic Indicators of Basic Early Literacy Skills (DIBELS) to assess Lauren's phonemic awareness skills. Lauren names seven initial sounds per minute on the assessment. The average score for Ms. Kelly's class is twenty-two initial sounds per minute. This places Lauren in the lowest 20% of the class achievement level in this assessment. In response to these data, Ms. Kelly requests a meeting with her school's Problem-Solving Team.

The team discusses Lauren's assessment results and her daily functioning in reading. They make note of the fact that Lauren had an eye exam before school began and no problems were indicated. The team recommends that Ms. Kelly or her teaching assistant work individually with Lauren to implement specific activities related to phonemic awareness from the *Rigby Literacy Reading Series.* Lauren will receive the individual instruction twice each week for twenty minutes per session. The team also requests that Lauren's progress be monitored once each week using the DIBELS. Ms. Kelly sets a goal of twenty initial sounds per minute to be achieved at the end of six weeks. Finally, the team sends home a parent questionnaire designed to gather information about Lauren's developmental history and functioning outside of the classroom.

Ms. Kelly's teaching assistant, Ms. James, implements the Tier One intervention as specified and administers the "Initial Sounds Fluency" portion of the DIBELS each Friday. After six weeks, Lauren has progressed to ten initial sounds per minute. The average for her class is now twenty-five initial sounds per minute. Lauren is now in the lowest 12% of her class achievement level in this assessment.

Ms. Kelly reports the data at the next Problem-Solving Team meeting. The team discusses Lauren's response to the intervention, including anecdotal information provided by Ms. James. Although Lauren has made progress, she is still far below her classmates, who are progressing at the expected rate. The team recommends implementation of a more intensive Tier Two intervention. In consultation with the literacy coach, the team recommends "Phonological Awareness Training for Reading," a scientifically validated reading program designed to increase phonological awareness. Lauren will receive instruction four times each week for twenty minutes per session. The sessions will be taught by the reading teacher or her teaching assistant. The teaching assistant will be trained to administer the program by the reading teacher and will be observed once each week during Lauren's lesson to ensure the program is being taught correctly and to make anecdotal notes of Lauren's progress. The DIBELS will be administered at the beginning of every other lesson.

Figure 3.3 presents these outcome data on phonemic awareness. At the end of fourteen weeks of intervention, Lauren's average score on the DIBELS Initial Sounds Fluency has increased to fifteen initial sounds per minute. Lauren was also administered the "Phoneme Segmentation Fluency" subtest and yielded a score of thirteen phoneme segments per minute. The average score for Ms. Kelly's class on this subtest is thirty-five phoneme segments per minute. The team meets again and determines that Lauren has not made significant progress as a result of the Tier Two intervention. The team discusses findings from the parent questionnaire as well. It is noted that Lauren was born prematurely at thirty-two weeks gestation and had a birth weight of Four pounds, six ounces. She stayed in neonatal intensive care for three weeks following birth. The team discusses these issues with the school nurse, who explains the possible links between these factors and poor school performance.

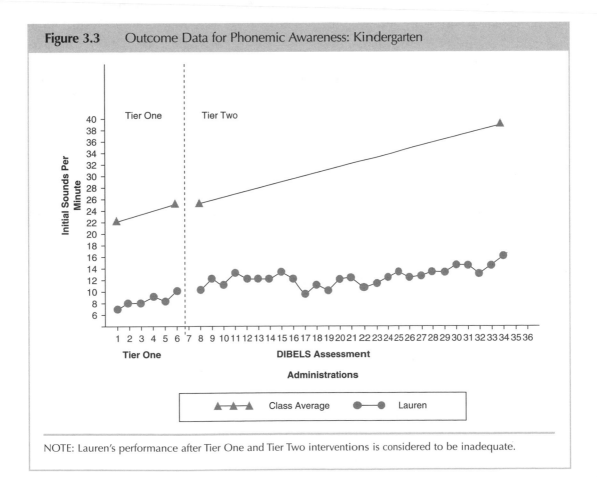

Figure 3.3　Outcome Data for Phonemic Awareness: Kindergarten

NOTE: Lauren's performance after Tier One and Tier Two interventions is considered to be inadequate.

Based on all information, the team recommends referral to Tier Three for further evaluation for special education services. Due process procedures are implemented and the school psychologist works with the team to begin the eligibility process. Also at this point, additional assessment for eligibility determination should be considered (Fuchs et al., 2003).

EXAMPLE TWO: MATH COMPUTATION: SIXTH GRADE

Nadia is a sixth-grade student who is having difficulty in math computation. Her math teacher, Mr. Hall, has determined that Nadia performs in the lowest 15% of the class, based on both grades and the state-wide assessment. After implementing a few simple strategies in the classroom, such as giving extra time on work and extra practice, Mr. Hall requests a meeting with the Problem-Solving Team. Based on Nadia's deficit areas identified through the group testing, the team recommends implementation of a Tier One intervention involving direct teaching of problem-solving strategies outlined in the basal math book, *Everyday Mathematics*, by McGraw-Hill Publishing. The instruction should take place in one forty-five minute segment each week in the general education classroom in individual or small-group settings. The team also recommends that Nadia's progress be monitored using curriculum-based assessment probes. A performance goal is set at 80% accuracy on word problems.

Mr. Hall utilizes tiered instruction, a strategy associated with differentiated instruction, to provide opportunities for small-group work in his classroom (Bender, 2005; Heacox, 2002; Tomlinson, 1999, 2003). In this strategy, students are pre-assessed to determine learning needs and placed in small groups according to their readiness levels for the particular skill to be taught. Students in each group are then given assignments that correspond to their functioning level; instruction is provided at a level slightly above their functioning level.

Mr. Hall administers a pre-test from the basal math book and groups his students according to ability. Nadia answers none of the five problems presented correctly, and she is placed into a group of six students whose functioning level is similar to her own. One day each week, all groups work on problem-solving activities that are appropriate to their functioning level. At the end of each lesson, students complete a five-minute math probe containing word problems. Mr. Hall develops the probes using tools found at www.interventioncentral.org. This Web site contains educational tools and downloads that are free to users. The "Curriculum-Based Measurement Warehouse" found on the site provides numerous curriculum-based assessments and a tool that allows teachers to design their own assessments.

After six weeks of small-group instruction, Nadia answers two of six problems correctly on the problem-solving probe. (See these data presented in Figure 3.4.) Mr. Hall discusses the intervention and Nadia's response with the Problem-Solving Team. The team recommends the implementation of a more intensive Tier Two strategy. The school's math coach, Ms. Ortega, recommends schema-based instruction, a research-based strategy shown to improve problem-solving skills for students (Bender, 2005; Chen, 1999; Fuchs et al., 2004). Ms. Ortega will co-teach with Mr. Hall for the first three sessions in order to demonstrate the strategy to him as well as to the students. She will visit the classroom in later sessions to observe for fidelity of instruction and to assist Mr. Hall with any questions he may have.

Schema-based instruction involves teaching students to categorize math problems into several general schemas according to the methods used to solve them (Bender, 2005). Students are taught the steps in solving problems based on these schema; when they encounter new problems, students determine the schema and use the same problem-solving method they have been previously taught. For complex problems requiring multiple operations, multiple schemas may be utilized to derive the correct answer, and students are taught how to apply multiple schemas in the correct order to solve the problem. Students are thus given guided and independent practice in identifying the schema and solving the problems. Research has shown this strategy to be effective, and, in using these story problem schema, students are able to transfer prior knowledge to new learning (Bender, 2005; Fuchs et al., 2004).

Mr. Hall implements the schema-based math computation strategy for twelve weeks in a tiered instruction group containing four students, all of whom performed poorly on the pre-test. As outlined by the Problem-Solving Team, he receives instruction and assistance from Mrs. Ortega for the first few weeks. Mr. Hall charts Nadia's progress on the probes administered at the beginning of each lesson (see Figure 3.4). Nadia has shown significant improvement in her problem-solving skills as evidenced by her last score of 100% correct. Mr. Hall reports Nadia's success to the team, and they jointly determine that Nadia no longer needs specific intervention strategies.

It is important to note in this example that, although the strategy was implemented specifically for Nadia's RTI, several other students also received the instruction on the schema-based computation strategy. In many cases, it is not necessary to implement individualized instruction for Tier One or Tier Two interventions, although individual monitoring of pupil progress is necessary. Still, if other students in the classroom are experiencing similar difficulties, they may still benefit from the strategy

Figure 3.4   Outcome Data for Math Computation: Sixth Grade

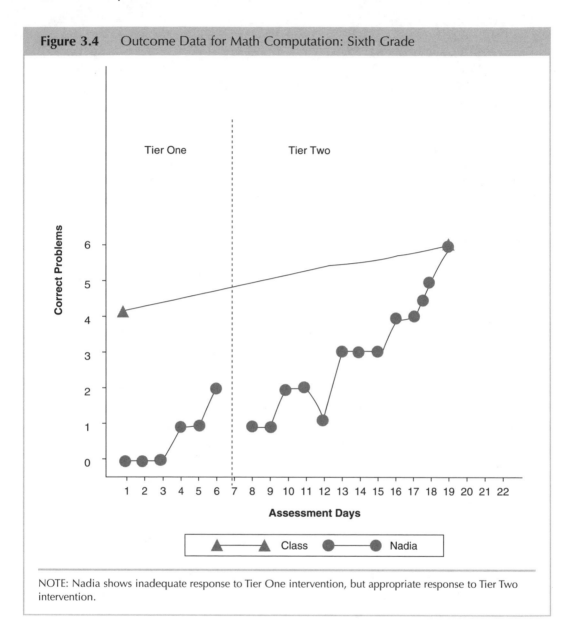

NOTE: Nadia shows inadequate response to Tier One intervention, but appropriate response to Tier Two intervention.

instruction even though they are not being considered for Tier One or Two interventions or for in-depth progress monitoring.

EXAMPLE THREE: AMERICAN HISTORY: TENTH GRADE

Jameel is a tenth-grade student who is experiencing extreme difficulty in American History. Jameel has struggled in content classes throughout middle and high school. He appears to be unmotivated. His teachers state that he never takes notes in class and rarely turns in assignments.

Mr. King, Jameel's American History teacher, believes that Jameel is capable of doing much better in his class. Mr. King spends time each day talking with Jameel about sports and other nonschool subjects. After a few weeks, when he feels he has established a good rapport with Jameel, Mr. King talks with Jameel about his school work. Together, they determine that Jameel is unable to glean and summarize important information from printed material and lectures. Because of that, he doesn't take notes and performs poorly on tests.

Mr. King and Jameel meet with the Problem-Solving Team to discuss strategies that will address these issues. The curriculum coordinator suggests teaching summarizing and note-taking strategies as described in *Classroom Instruction That Works* (Marzano, Norford, Paynter, Pickering, & Gaddy, 2001; Marzano, Pickering, & Pollock, 2001). The strategies outlined in these books have a strong research base and will generalize into many content areas. Mr. King decides to implement the use of summary frames. In this strategy, students are given "frame questions" to guide their reading and assist them in understanding text. The questions are specific to different types of expository writing (e.g., narrative, argumentation, problem or solution, conversation, etc.). The teacher takes standard questions for each type of writing and adjusts them as needed to fit the text. The student then uses the questions as a guided reading tool while reading content material (Marzano et al., p. 63).

Jameel agrees to work with Mr. King for ten minutes two days each week at the end of his lunch period. During this time, Mr. King will provide him with a summary frame to use during the next day's assignment. Jameel agrees to try the strategy and seems excited to have extra help.

On that basis, Mr. King implements the strategy for five weeks. During that time, he administers weekly testing consisting of questions similar to those that will be on the final exam. He shares the results with Jameel and together they chart Jameel's progress and develop goals for the next week. Figure 3.5 illustrates Jameel's progress over the five-week interval. Jameel shows marked improvement on his understanding of content material. Jameel is also turning in more assignments each week. Mr. King presents the outcome data to the team, and the team decides to continue use of the strategy in Mr. King's classroom. Because Jameel experiences similar problems in other classes, the team recommends that the literature teacher implement the strategy as well.

FINAL THOUGHTS

The examples presented in this chapter describe interventions at different grade levels. We chose these varying levels to illustrate that RTI can be

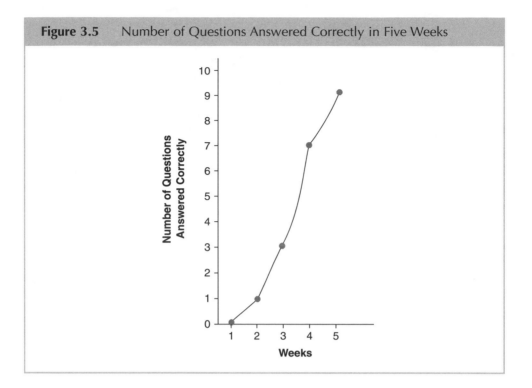

Figure 3.5 Number of Questions Answered Correctly in Five Weeks

implemented with any student at any time. Although most of the current research has focused on instruction in the elementary grades, the findings can be generalized and applied to instruction in middle and secondary grades. Progress monitoring in the upper grades is most often completed based on teacher-made assessment tools or assessments that come standard with textbooks. Interventions may be more closely related to learning strategies than to specific reading or math skills. Otherwise, the process is the same regardless of the student's age.

We want to once again stress the importance of providing a structured format for the problem-solving model. Teachers must make decisions based on student data. Resources, both human and material, must be available to provide guidance and training in research-based strategies. This often involves reallocation of existing resources, such as providing math and literacy coaches in schools to train in the strategies. Each school and system should develop a comprehensive plan for providing these resources. In order to provide assistance to school districts in developing effective procedures in these areas, we have provided guidelines to streamline the problem-solving RTI in Table 3.2.

Table 3.2   Guidelines for Streamlining the Problem-Solving RTI

1. The variable nature of problem-solving RTIs requires districts to provide extensive and ongoing staff development in areas such as the decision-making model, progress monitoring, and research-based strategies in content areas and behavior.

2. Resources that give teachers access to research-based interventions, both within and outside of the district, should be identified. Examples include literacy and math coaches, behavioral consultants, curriculum consultants, and regional educational agency representatives. The Web sites and additional resources presented in this book will also be helpful.

3. Easy-to-use, nonrepetitive forms for teams to use in their documentation should be provided. Also, the forms presented in Appendix D may be edited for this application.

NOTE: In Table 2.3, we provided guidelines for streamlining the standard treatment protocol RTI. Those same recommendations apply for problem-solving RTI. In addition to those recommendations, we offer additional suggestions that pertain directly to the problem-solving model.

REFERENCES

Bender, W. N. (2005). *Differentiating Math Instruction: Strategies that work for K–8 classrooms* (pp. 34–39). Thousand Oaks, CA: Corwin Press.

Chen, Z. (1999). Schema induction in children's analogical problem solving. *Journal of Educational Psychology, 91,* 703–715.

Colorado Department of Education Exceptional Student Services Unit (2005, September). *Indicators of school readiness for RTI self-assessment tool.* Denver, CO: Colorado Department of Education.

Deno, S. (2002). Problem solving as "best practice." In A. Thomas & J. Grimes (Eds.), *Best practices in school psychology*—(Vol. IV, pp. 37–56). Bethesda, MD: National Association of School Psychologists.

Deno, S., Grimes, J., Reschly, D., & Schrag, J. (2001). *Minneapolis Public Schools— Problem solving model: Review team report.* Unpublished paper.

Flugum, K. R., & Reschly, D. J. (1994). Prereferral interventions: Quality indices and outcomes. *Journal of School Psychology, 32*(1), 1–14.

Fuchs, L. S. (2003). Assessing intervention responsiveness: Conceptual and technical issues. *Learning Disabilities Research & Practice, 18*(3), 172–186.

Fuchs, D., Fuchs, L. S., McMaster, K. L., Yen, L., & Svenson, E. (2004). Nonresponders: How to find them?. How to help them?. What do they mean for special education?. *TEACHING Exceptional Children, 36*(6), 72–77.

Fuchs, L. S., Fuchs, D., Prentice, K., Hamlett, C., Finelli, R., & Courey, S. (2004). Enhancing mathematical problem solving among third-grade students with schema-based instruction. *Journal of Educational Psychology, 96*(4), 635–647.

Fuchs, D., Mock, D., Morgan, P. L., & Young, C. L. (2003). Responsiveness-to-Intervention: Definitions, evidence, and implications for the learning disabilities construct. *Learning Disabilities Research & Practice, 18*(3), 157–171.

Grimes, J., & Kurns, S. (2003, December). *An intervention-based system for addressing NCLB and IDEA expectations: A multiple tiered model to ensure every child learns.* Paper presented at the National Research Center on Learning Disabilities Responsiveness-to-Intervention Symposium, Kansas City, MO.

Hall, S. L. (2006). *I've DIBEL'd, now what?* New York: Sopris West Educational Services.

Heacox, D. (2002). Differentiating instruction in the regular classroom: How to reach and teach all learners, grades 3-12. Minneapolis, MN: Free Spirit Publishing.

Marston, D., Muyskens, P., Lau, M., & Canter, A. (2003). Problem-solving model for decision making with high-incidence disabilities: The Minneapolis experience. *Learning Disabilities Research & Practice, 18*(3), 187–200.

Marzano, R. J., Norford, J. S., Paynter, D. E., Pickering, D. J., & Gaddy, B. B. (2001). *A handbook for classroom instruction that works.* Alexandria, VA: Association for Supervision and Curriculum Development.

Marzano, R., Pickering, D., & Pollock, J. (2001). *Classroom instruction that works.* Alexandria, VA: Association for Supervision and Curriculum Development.

Maslow, A., & Lowery, R. (Eds.). (1998). *Toward a psychology of being* (3rd ed.). New York: John Wiley.

Minneapolis Public Schools. (2002, December). *Identification of students with disability under the problem-solving model.* Retrieved August 16, 2006, from http://pic .mpls.k12.mn.us

Minneapolis Public Schools. (2006). *Performance assessment of academic skills in the problem solving model.* Retrieved August 16, 2006, from http://pic.mpls.k12 .mn.us

Speece, D. L., Case, L. P., & Molloy, D. E. (2003). Responsiveness to general education instruction as the first gate to learning disabilities identification. *Learning Disabilities Research & Practice, 18*(3), 147–156.

Tilley, W. D. (2003, December). *How many tiers are needed for successful prevention and early intervention? Heartland Area Education Agency's evolution from four to three tiers.* Paper presented at the National Research Center on Learning Disabilities Responsiveness-to-Intervention Symposium, Kansas City, MO.

Tomlinson, C. A. (1999). *The differentiated classroom: Responding to the needs of all learners.* Alexandria, VA: Association for Supervision and Curriculum Development.

Tomlinson, C. A. (2003). *Fulfilling the promise of the differentiated classroom: Strategies and tools for responsive teaching.* Alexandria, VA: Association for Supervision and Curriculum Development.

4

Implementing RTI to Meet the Needs of All Learners

Cara Shores, Victor Morgan, and
William N. Bender

In the previous chapters, we have discussed standard protocol and problem-solving models for RTI and have provided examples for implementing each model. Although we have discussed RTI in the context of determining eligibility of students for learning disability services, we believe that the emphasis on RTI is much broader, and will impact every single teacher and child in the nation. Thus, implementation of RTI in general education classrooms across this nation will result in enhanced instruction for all students. In an era in which schools are searching for ways to achieve adequate yearly progress toward increasingly demanding educational standards, RTI will offer a renewed emphasis on "best practice" instruction for all students. By using RTI, teachers will be more equipped than ever before to demonstrate the exact achievement levels of their students, and to tailor instruction directly toward any identified academic deficits. Further, because both general education teachers and special education teachers will be heavily involved in RTI interventions in the first two tiers, all teachers will become much more fluent in this instructional practice.

Perhaps the single biggest advantage of implementing RTI is the fact that RTI results in increased understanding of the academic skills of each student in the class. Throughout this book, we have discussed the importance of getting to know and understand our students and their different abilities and skill levels; this is consistent with various other recommendations in the field of education. Carol Ann Tomlinson, for example, in her groundbreaking work on differentiated instruction (Tomlinson, 1999), suggests that teachers should study their own students. Even more significant, Dr. James Comer, creator of The Comer Process and professor at Yale University, proposes that no significant learning occurs without a significant relationship (Payne, 2005). Both researchers and practitioners in education now understand that the quality of a student's relationship with a teacher has the most direct and significant effect on the student's involvement in learning. All of this lends credence to our belief that meaningful learning for all students occurs through positive and supportive relationships with caring and nurturing adults. For these reasons, this chapter stresses the relationships teachers should strive to develop with various subgroups of students in the class.

In this chapter, the focus is on culturally and linguistically diverse learners, many of whom are overrepresented in the population of students classified as learning disabled. In particular, we will focus on English language learners, because several aspects of RTI implementation may differentially affect this group. Further, other subgroups of students will be discussed in this context—including culturally diverse students and students living in poverty—because these groups may likewise be affected by implementation of RTI. We will explore the issue of disproportionate placement in special education for each of these subgroups. We will then provide specific strategies designed to address these factors and concerns.

ENGLISH LANGUAGE LEARNERS

The population of speakers of other languages in America has increased dramatically over the past fifteen to twenty years. According to the U.S. Census Bureau, 18% of the U.S. population (approximately forty-seven million people) speaks a language other than English at home. More than half of those individuals speak Spanish as their primary language. The next largest groups in this category speak Chinese, French, and German. There were 380 total categories of languages or language families reported on the 2000 census as being primary languages in homes (U.S. Census Bureau, 2003).

Compounding the diversity in language, the distribution of these individuals is not equal across the country. When examining the number of individuals who speak a language other than English at home, 29% live in the West, 20% in the Northeast, 15% in the South, and 9% in the Midwest, with the others scattered in various other states. The largest concentrations of non-English-speaking individuals are in California (39%), New Mexico (37%), Texas (31%), New York (28%), Hawaii (27%), Arizona (26%), and New Jersey (25%). The largest increases in this population from 1990 to 2000 occurred in Nevada (an increase of 193%) and in Georgia (an increase of 164%), according to recent data from the U.S. Census Bureau (2003).

When applied to our public school system, these figures are somewhat startling. In public schools, these students are referred to as English language learners (ELLs). ELLs are those students who speak a language other than English and are learning English (National Council for Teachers of English, 2006, p. 1). In the 2003–04 school year, there were reportedly over five million English language learners in U.S. schools. This represents a 65% increase over the previous ten years. English language proficiency among these students ranges from no English to fully proficient. Spanish is spoken by 82% of the English language learners, but over 350 languages are spoken by school-aged children (National Council for Teachers of English, 2006). Further, Hispanic learners are the fastest growing ethnic group and largest minority group in U.S. schools (U.S. Census Bureau, as cited in Klingner & Artiles, 2003).

This increase has made a dramatic impact on American education. Researchers and practitioners alike have searched for the best ways to teach English language learners, resulting in a great deal of debate and, occasionally, controversy. Because of the wide range of ability among ELLs, it is often difficult to determine which services are needed for individual students. As mentioned earlier, there is a heavy concentration of English language learners in certain parts of the country and, specifically, in certain states. Schools in these areas must provide language services to large numbers of students at varying levels of proficiency. In other areas, such as the Midwest, schools might have only one student who speaks a particular language. This brings about an entirely different set of issues and needs for the student; the impact of RTI may be more profound for this group of students than for others in the school.

DISPROPORTIONALITY IN SPECIAL EDUCATION

One critical factor facing educators throughout the United States is that of disproportionate representation in special education programs. In many school districts throughout the country, this is the case for some subgroups of English language learners and for culturally and ethnically diverse students, in particular, African American students. Disproportionality occurs through overrepresentation of subgroups of children in certain disability categories and underrepresentation in other areas.

There are no clear figures of disproportionality for English language learners as a whole because information at the federal level does not address language proficiency. Instead, we have data on ethnic groups who typically are composed of ELLs. For example, Hispanic or Latino students (representing the largest group of English language learners) have been consistently underrepresented in gifted education programs (Hosp & Reschly, 2004).

Overrepresentation of Hispanic students in LD has also been reported (President's Commission on Excellence in Special Education, 2002), revealing significant overrepresentation of Hispanic children in LD (Donovan & Cross, 2002; Reschly & Hosp, 2004; Scruggs & Mastriopieri, 2002). As one example, Klingner and Artiles (2003) reported that there is evidence of overrepresentation of English language learners as a group in high-incidence disability categories in California. There is also evidence that Hispanic students are overrepresented in certain other disability categories in which some professional judgment is used in the eligibility procedures (e.g., categories such as behavior disorders), but not in non-judgmental categories which would include, for example, auditory, visual, or orthopedic impairment (Donovan & Cross, 2002).

Another subgroup that is significantly overrepresented in special education is African American children. More than 2.2 million African American students are receiving special education services in schools across the United States (U. S. Department of Education, 2002). According to the National Research Council, more than 14% of African American students are in special education, as compared to 13% of American Indian students, 12% of White students, 11% of Hispanic students, and 5% of Asian American students (Paolino, 2003). African American students are also three times as likely as Caucasian students to be labeled mentally retarded, two times as likely to be labeled emotionally disturbed, and 1.3 times as likely to be labeled as having a learning disability (Council for Exceptional Children [CEC], 2002). According to the National Institute for Urban School Improvement (2001), African Americans are significantly overrepresented in the two special education categories of high incidence—learning disabilities and emotional/behavior disorders (Oswald, Coutinho, Best, & Nguyen, 2001).

Fierros & Conroy (2002) report that once identified, students of color, especially African American and Latino/Hispanic students, are more likely than Caucasian students to be placed in restrictive educational settings. The U. S. Department of Education's (2002) report indicates that only 37% of African Americans, compared to 43% of Hispanic students and 55% of White students, are provided access to inclusive educational settings (in that report, inclusion is defined as less than 21% of the school day out of the general education classroom). However, African American students (33%) and Hispanic students (28%) are more likely to spend more than 60% of the school day outside of the general education classroom (e.g., separate class, separate school, and residential facilities), meaning less time in the general education class, less time with peers, and reduced access to the general curriculum (Fierros & Conroy, 2002). Furthermore, African American students are suspended and expelled at higher rates (Ishii-Jordan, 1997) and have higher dropout rates (U. S. Department of Education, 2002).

Finally, we look at the subgroup of children living in poverty. Although children from poverty are not classified as a subgroup when considering disproportionality, poverty is a reality for many students. In 2006, the poverty rate for children under the age of five was 20.2%; for children under eighteen, the rate was 17.1% (U.S. Census Bureau, 2006). Students living in poverty are more likely to experience school failure than children who do not live in poverty (Payne, 2005). This may be due to multiple factors, including low education level of parents, living in single-parent families, and limited access to early educational resources (Apiwattanalunggarn & Luster, 2005). As a result, children from poverty often do not have the cognitive strategies or methods of processing information necessary to be successful in school (Payne, 2005). We will explore the interaction of poverty and the overrepresentation of culturally and linguistically diverse groups in the next section.

FACTORS CONTRIBUTING TO DISPROPORTIONALITY

There are several factors that may contribute to disproportionality of the aforementioned subgroups, especially in the issue of overrepresentation of students with learning disabilities. One factor that relates specifically to English language learners may be the lack of consistency in applying the language exclusionary clause to eligibility determinations. IDEA (2004) requires that eligibility teams determine if a student's academic deficits are the result of Limited English Proficiency (see Federal Regulations of the U.S. Office of Education, 300.309[a][3][vi]). If the learning problems are found to be language related, the student should not be labeled learning disabled. However, there is some question as to how well this stipulation is applied in eligibility determinations. Results from a survey of school psychologists indicated that most did not carefully consider language acquisition and years of instruction in English when determining whether students had adequate opportunity to learn (Ochoa, Rivera, & Powell, 1997).

IDEA 2004 also requires eligibility teams to rule out environmental or economic disadvantage as a possible explanation for learning problems. Practitioners often find it extremely difficult to apply this exclusionary clause due to the fact that so many factors are interrelated. For example, children who are immigrants are twice as likely to be poor than children born in the United States (Payne, 2005). Thirty-four percent of African American children under the age of eighteen live in poverty (U. S. Census Bureau, 2006). The fact that they are poor may be the key reason that these students are at risk for failure. Indeed, children from middle-class Black families academically outperform poor children, regardless of ethnicity (Hodgkinson, 1995). However, the overwhelming majority of African American children come from single-parent households; this negatively impacts the overall average income level in these homes. Further, African Americans work longer hours for a lesser amount of money than their White counterparts earn (Toppo, 2000); frequently, they are minimally educated and have substantial limitations on their time. We should also consider that children raised in poverty frequently experience consistent exposure to English that would not be considered "Standard English." This may include many children in Appalachia and children living in the old historic settlements known as the "Sea Islands" along the U. S. south-eastern coast, inner-city children, children in the Louisiana bayou country, and other groups of students living in poverty in various regions of the country. It is the interaction of all these factors that makes application of exclusionary clauses so difficult.

Another factor to consider is the potential bias in educational and intelligence testing (Klingner & Artiles, 2003; President's Commission on Excellence in Special Education, 2002; Stanovich, 1999). As discussed in previous chapters, dissatisfaction over the IQ/achievement discrepancy model has been well documented in the literature; this dissatisfaction has provided the driving force behind the RTI initiative (Fletcher et al., 1994; Vellutino, Scanlon, Small, & Fanuele, 2006). However, when we consider the problems with discrepancies in relation to the practice of testing culturally diverse students, more specific arguments arise. The test performance of linguistically diverse students may be influenced by differences in interpretation of questions and lack of vocabulary knowledge (Garcia & Pearson 1994; Klingner & Artiles, 2003). These interpretive differences are certainly culturally influenced, resulting in highly questionable IQ and achievement scores. This may in turn result in underestimation of the learning potential of English language learners and/or minority students.

In a study spanning more than ten years, researchers compared students' 1972 IQ scores with their 1982 standardized test scores. When students' achievement scores were higher than indicated by their IQ scores, they were labeled as overachievers. In this study, Hispanic students who performed poorly on the IQ test were more likely than Caucasian students to achieve above expected levels. The researchers concluded that utilizing IQ scores for decision making resulted in inaccurate decisions and predictions for Hispanic students (Klingner & Artiles, 2003; Valdez & Figueroa, 1994). This sometimes results in lowered expectations and "tracking" into lower-level classes, a factor that has also been noted relative to African American students.

Another factor in disproportionality is the lack of research and practices designed specifically to include subgroups such as English language learners or African American students. Most of the extant research does not involve these populations; as a result, most policy decisions made relative to special education placement and instruction are based on what we know about Caucasian children with English as their first language (Vaughn, Mathes, Linan-Thompson, & Francis, 2005). In particular, there are few studies available related to instructional strategies appropriate for students who are not proficient in English. As a result, current prereferral interventions may be inadequate in quality, intensity, and/or number for ELLs (Carrasquillo & Rodriguez, 1997; Klingner & Artiles, 2003). Although some researchers are addressing this issue—for example, Dr. Sharon Vaughn and her colleagues at University of Texas at Austin are conducting ongoing research on Spanish-speaking students—there is a clear need for much more research on all educational issues dealing with ELLs and ethnically diverse students (Vaughn et al., 2005, 2006). In the view of some researchers, the chief issue with disproportionality is not the number of culturally and linguistically diverse students in special education, but the reasoning and procedures used in order to refer, evaluate, and place them there (Donovan & Cross, 2002; Vaughn & Fuchs, 2003). Under the current procedures for identifying learning problems, most students are selected for evaluation based on teacher referrals. These referrals are often supported by subjective comments rather than objective data. For example, a teacher may refer a student for evaluation because he believes the student has had sufficient time to learn English and yet has not made sufficient progress. There may be no consideration of proficiency in the primary language, quality of instruction in English, or other cultural and personal issues that have a direct impact on student achievement for English language learners. The same may be applicable for African American students. Instruction for students from various subcultures may be based on a curriculum that seems to have no relevance for that subcultural group. Lower teacher expectations, a disproportionate percentage of "left-brain" lesson plans, tracking, and negative peer pressure have also been cited as reasons for poor achievement among students of color (Kunjufu,

2002). In turn, failure to consider these factors often yields a biased picture of students' performance and capabilities.

Reflection 4.1 **Disproportionality in Your School or School System**

Does your school or school system have groups of students who are disproportionately placed in special education? You can find out by following these steps. First, you should obtain information on the general population in your school district. Next, you should identify the specific subgroups in your school and ascertain how many from each group are currently in special education. You should also seek information on the eligibility categories in which they are found. You can then discuss the issue of disproportionality in your school. If your school data demonstrate such a concern, you should list various factors that may have caused the disproportionate placements, and then identify strategies to address these issues.

The question of why African American students are placed in special education in disproportionate numbers speaks to the uniqueness of African American students, as well as to educators' ignorance of the subcultural issues facing this population. Reasons for overidentification for special education include:

a. Difficulty in constructing instructional programs that address students' unique learning strengths and needs;

b. The opportunities students have, or have not, had to learn;

c. Disconnection in most schools between the race, culture, and class of teachers and that of their students;

d. High reliance on high-stakes assessment; and

e. A great disparity between a cultural/familial interpretation of a child's behavior and the school's interpretation of that behavior (CEC, 2002; Grossman, 1985; Ishii-Jordan, 1997; National Institute for Urban School Improvement, 2001).

Viewed together, these are "system" failures that must be addressed at the systemic level. That is, the quandary does not rest in the child alone or within individual faculty; rather, the school as a system is responsible for the African American student's learning and, as a result, must deal with the child's unique and distinctive needs.

From the work of the states and various organizations such as the National Center for Culturally Responsive Educational Systems, a common framework for action to address disproportionality is emerging. The framework involves three components:

1. increasing the number of schools using effective literacy and behavioral interventions for students who are culturally and linguistically diverse,

2. decreasing inappropriate referral to special education, and

3. increasing the use of prevention and early intervention strategies.

These three components are part of the rationale and purpose behind the use of a responsiveness to intervention model (National Center for Culturally Responsive Educational Systems, 2006). Thus RTI may assist educators to more adequately formulate effective instructional programs for these groups of students.

THE IMPACT OF RTI ON DISPROPORTIONALITY FOR ENGLISH LANGUAGE LEARNERS

Proponents of RTI suggest that disproportionality will be much less prevalent when RTI is implemented because, under RTI, eligibility and placement decisions are based on student-achievement data rather than on teacher referrals (Batsche et al., 2006). However, we must still exercise caution in working with all at-risk learners. Teachers often may not understand or consider the implications of the factors noted here, or the components of the framework mentioned previously. Thus it is clear that disproportionate placement can still occur today (National Center for Culturally Responsive Educational Systems, 2005). Therefore, in order to address concerns for English language learners, we must consider several key factors that influence their achievement, including differences among ELLs, elements of second language acquisition, first language effect on second language, and influence of cultural and environmental issues. We will examine each of these issues as they relate to the implementation of RTI.

English language learners, as well as other ethnically diverse groups, are often viewed as a generic population possessing many common characteristics. Although it is true that there are similarities among most members of the population, there are also vast differences between them. Consider, for example, subgroups within the Spanish-speaking population. Children from southern Texas with Mexican ancestry demonstrate a slightly different language and will certainly have a vastly different cultural experience than children from Miami, Florida, many of whom stem from Cuban ancestry. Both of these groups of children may be different from Hispanic students in east Los Angeles, California. In another example, African American children from the Deep South will certainly exhibit a different language experience and subculture from African American children from inner-city Chicago or New York. Based on these differences, it is clearly inaccurate to consider any subgroup—ELLs, Hispanic children, or African American children—as a singular monolithic group.

Freeman and Freeman (2004) gave examples of three types of English language learners identified in earlier research. They are long-term English learners, learners with limited formal schooling, and English language learners who are proficient in their native language.

Long-Term English Learners

The long-term English learner is defined as a student who speaks English and no longer receives ELL services in the school setting, but still has numerous academic difficulties. Many of these students have had most or all of their formal education in American schools. They may be proficient in conversational English, but have not developed the language skills necessary to be successful in content area classes. Language-acquisition theory (e.g., Cummins, 1980) states that English language learners must become proficient in language at two levels: basic interpersonal communication skills (conversational English) and cognitive academic language proficiency (academic English). According to the theory, two years are required for mastery of conversational English, but five to seven years are necessary for students to become proficient in academic English (Cummins, 1980). Further, academic language must be coupled with academic content knowledge for learning to occur in various subject areas. In order for these students to achieve, teachers must provide background knowledge and instruction that is rich in contextual cues (Saenz, Fuchs, & Fuchs, 2005; National Council for Teachers of English, 2006).

Teachers unaware of these background knowledge deficits among their students, however, may not recognize the academic language deficit. They may assume that, because the student can speak English conversationally, he or she can understand and benefit from instruction in English. When that student subsequently experiences learning problems, it is often attributed to other factors rather than a language-acquisition problem, and may result in a placement in special education.

Learners With Limited Schooling

The second type of English language learners, those with limited formal schooling, may be new arrivals to the United States or may have had their education interrupted. Alternatively, they may move seasonally, and thereby experience many such interruptions in their education, such as children from migrant worker families. These students are not fluent in conversational English. Moreover, they may not have developed proficiency at the academic level in either their native language or in English. It is not uncommon for these students to enroll in school knowing no English at all. Because of this, they will struggle in school and require a great deal of support (Klingner & Artiles, 2003).

Learners Proficient in Their Native Language But Not in English

Last, we have English language learners who are proficient in their native language at both the conversational and academic levels. Although these students may have limited or no English, these students have demonstrated language learning capability. In fact, numerous studies have shown that certain skills in the native language are predictive of second language acquisition (Cummins, 1979; Lindsey, Manis, & Bailey, 2003; National Council for Teachers of English, 2006). Cummins's linguistic interdependence hypothesis states that there is a direct impact of the level of proficiency for the first language when the student begins learning the second language. Along those lines, Vaughn et al. (2006) summarized findings from several researchers, showing that phonological processing, decoding skills, and verbal activities are good predictors of reading success and Response to Intervention in both English and Spanish instruction. Although these specific skills may not transfer into languages other then Spanish, Cummins's theory suggests that first language proficiency would still be a critical factor. Because of this relationship, this type of learner may have less difficulty becoming proficient in English than learners with limited schooling (Klingner & Artiles, 2003).

In planning RTI interventions, as well as other instructional activities, it is important for teachers to understand these differences among ELLs. Each type of student needs to be instructed differently. Each will vary significantly in the amount of time required to obtain fluency in conversational and academic English. Support will be required at different levels and with different resources. Without consideration of these factors, students may be determined to be nonresponsive to interventions based on misleading data. For that reason, it is imperative that teachers learn as much as they can about their students. As we discussed in Chapter 3, background and personal information should serve as vital components in the decision-making process. Table 4.1 contains guidance in the types of information that should be obtained for English language learners prior to making decisions regarding student progress.

Table 4.1 Information to Consider for English Language Learners

Language Experience and ELL Services

- First language
- Length of time in U.S. schools
- Language proficiency and/or diagnostic screening scores
- Time, duration, and description of ELL services
- Student fluency in first language: conversational and/or academic
- Student fluency in second language: conversational and/or academic
- Primary language in home
- Data of progress while receiving ELL services
- Instructional accommodations in all curriculum areas
- Quantity and quality of instruction in first language
- Quantity and quality of instruction in second language

Educational Experience

- Amount, location, and description of formal education in first language
- Time elapsed during transition between native land and U.S. schools
- Number and location of schools attended in United States

Family Considerations

- Parents' ability to communicate with school/teacher
- Parents' ability to communicate with child
- Student's age at time of migration
- Changes in socioeconomic status from homeland
- Close family member (parent or sibling) remaining in homeland
- Whether student lives with adult other than biological parent
- Psychological stresses related to migration
- Untreated illnesses or disease
- Fears
- Unusual/problematic behavior patterns

SOURCE: These considerations came from a variety of sources, including the authors, as well as Marler and Sanchez-Lopez (2006).

It is imperative for teams to determine the student's level of English proficiency at both the conversational and academic levels. It should never be assumed that conversational proficiency indicates academic proficiency. It is also very important for teams to determine the student's level of fluency in their native language. They should gather as much information as possible about the student's academic history and functioning prior to coming to the United States. Indications of learning problems that occurred in the native language should serve as a red flag that current problems may involve more than language acquisition. Again, Table 4.1 provides guidance in the types of information needed to make appropriate decisions.

RTI does indeed hold promise as a better way to identify English language learners with disabilities. However, school systems must take specific actions to address the issues raised here, as noted below.

- Teachers must be trained in appropriate strategies and interventions proven effective for working with English language learners, which means more research must be conducted (Hosp & Reschly, 2004; Vaughn & Fuchs, 2003).
- Teachers should also receive training in theory of second language acquisition (Freeman & Freeman, 2004).
- Decision-making teams must consider classroom observations as an important part of their data, and use them to determine quality of instruction as it relates to ELLs. Certainly, a person knowledgeable about the instruction of English language learners and the requirements and implications of the exclusionary clause should be present in all decision-making meetings (Klingner & Artiles, 2003).
- Finally, resources—both human and material—must be allocated to support teachers and students in this area. Clearly, good resources at the school can greatly assist in providing such background knowledge. Teachers should carefully consider the available resources in their school for planning instruction for children learning English.

Reflection 4.2	Resources for Teaching English Language Learners

Teaching students who are learning English as a second language can be a daunting task. The more instructional resources you have at hand, the more likely you are to succeed with diverse learners. What resources do you have available to provide support for you and your ELL students? Is there a full-time ESOL teacher at your school? Are appropriate instructional materials available in the child's primary language? Are additional resources available in the media center and/or at other schools in the district? As a part of this reflective activity, you might wish to list these materials prior to beginning your year with an ELL student. Remember to list all resources you find, because you can never really tell what resources you might need later in the year. Also, it may be helpful to explore national resources. These Web sites might be helpful to you.

National Council for Teachers of English:
http://www.ncte.org

Center for Expansion of Language and Thinking:
http://www.ed.arizona.edu/celt/fs7.html

Teachers of English Speakers of Other Languages:
http://www.tesol.org

Office of English Language Acquisition, Language Enhancement and Academic Achievement for Limited English Proficient Students (OELA):
http://www.ncela.gwu.edu/oela/

Everything ESL:
http://www.everythingesl.net

Illinois Resource Center:
http://www.thecenterweb.org

Mora's Modules:
http://coe/sdsu.edu/people/jmora/MoraModules/Default.htm

THE IMPACT OF RTI ON DISPROPORTIONALITY FOR AFRICAN AMERICAN STUDENTS AND CHILDREN IN POVERTY

Educators, advocates, and practitioners in the field of cultural and linguistic education suggest that RTI is an exceptional model for addressing the needs of culturally and linguistically diverse learners and students living in poverty. However, this is the case only if the many classroom procedures and interventions that are appropriate for these populations are implemented with fidelity. For example, a significantly large percentage of students in these populations seem to be right-brained learners (Kunjufu, 2002), and such learners may require more varied instructional activities that emphasize these right-brain learning strengths. (See Sousa, 2006, pp. 165–212 for a discussion of these activities.) By way of explanation, left-brained learners/thinkers are generally very logical, sequential, rational, and organized thinkers. Right-brained learner/thinkers, on the other hand, are disorganized, nonsequential, nonlogical thinkers (Hale, 1986, 2001; Kunjufu, 2002). They are often creative and may be quite imaginative. Such right-brained individuals may be somewhat more artistic and/or musically inclined. Also, right-brained thinkers perform better with multiple stimuli and little or more noise (Hale, 1986, 2001; Kunjufu, 2002). Because of the focus on linguistic-based, left-brain activities in most classrooms, some have suggested that educators may not accommodate and/or plan as effectively for students that demonstrate these right-brain learning strengths (Kunjufu, 2002).

Further, many African American students prefer more kinesthetic/tactile learning (Kunjufu, 2002). African American children are generally more kinesthetic than their Caucasian counterparts and these students have a higher level of motor activity (Hale, 2001). African American learners and students in poverty, particularly boys, have difficulty sitting for long periods of time without the opportunity to expend some of their energy. Therefore, classroom learning activities should be designed to ensure that these students have the opportunity to move around.

To improve the education of African American students, teacher education programs must excel in preparing teachers and administrators who have an elevated level of authentic knowledge of African American culture; a deeper understanding of the impact African American culture has on behavior, learning styles, and preferred teaching styles; and a genuine appreciation for the valuable repertoire of experiences African American students bring to school (Hale, 2006; Kunjufu, 2002). Table 4.2 provides numerous strategies to address the learning differences typical of African American students.

Reflection 4.3	Resources for Teaching Students Who Live in Poverty

It is often difficult for teachers, most of whom have middle-class backgrounds, to understand the culture of poverty. Yet, research shows that individuals living in poverty differ from middle-class individuals in numerous ways including language structure, values, family structure, and levels of independence. This often leads to conflict when children from this culture are placed into a middle-class educational setting (Payne, 2005). Do you teach students who live in significant poverty? If so, you might find the following resources helpful in understanding and teaching your students:

Payne, R. K. (2005). *A framework for understanding poverty*. Highlands, TX: aha! Process, Inc.

aha! Process, Inc.: Eye-Opening Learning: http://www.ahaprocess.com

EXAMPLE: FOURTH-GRADE READING FOR AN ENGLISH LANGUAGE LEARNER

Here is an example of an RTI process for an English language learner. You will notice that it is somewhat different from the examples given in Chapters 2 and 3; for ELL students we recommend a process that is somewhat of a blend of the standard protocol and problem-solving approaches. The actual intervention involves the standard protocol, but the problem-solving process is used to address the related factors that may be affecting the student's performance. A problem-solving discussion is necessary to determine if the student's learning problems are related to language acquisition, external factors, or a learning disability; thus, for this type of learner we recommended this blended approach.

Manuel is in fourth grade. He was born in Mexico City, Mexico, where he lived until he was eight years old. Two years ago, Manuel's family moved to the United States. He entered second grade at Park Street Elementary, the school he is currently attending. Park Street Elementary has a growing Hispanic population, currently 14% of the total school population.

Manuel is struggling with all academic classes. His teacher, Mrs. Lovett, is concerned that he is losing interest in school and doesn't seem

Table 4.2 Strategies for Teaching African American Students and Students From Poverty

- *Increase attention to writing and its relationship to reading.* Culturally and linguistically diverse students should write every day. The writing should be grounded in the ongoing activities of the classroom and interests of individual students. Students are helped to see their writing through the entire process of prewriting, drafting, revising, editing, and publishing (Forman & Conroy, 1992; Shanahan, 1990, as cited in Strickland, 1994)

- *Provide greater student choice in what students read and write in the classroom.* Teachers should encourage students to share in the decision making regarding choice of topics to write about and materials to read (Calkins, 1986, Cambourne, 1987, and Wells, 1986, as cited in Strickland, 1994).

- *Provide greater integration of oral language and literacy across all subjects in the curriculum.* Literacy learning is viewed as a key element of every aspect of the curriculum. Reading, writing, speaking, listening, and reasoning are integral to every subject throughout the day (Lipson, Valencia, Wixson, & Peters, 1993, and Pappas, Ouler, Barry, & Rassel, 1993, as cited in Strickland, 1994).

- *Design learning activities to enable children to move as they learn.* African American students are generally more kinesthetic than Caucasian students and have a higher level of motor activity (Hale, 2001). African American students, particularly boys, should not be required to sit for long periods of time without an opportunity to expend energy.

- *Orient learning toward people rather than toward objects.* African American families exhibit a strong affective orientation in child rearing (Ellison, Boykin, Towns, & Stokes, 2000). Most African American students will respond best when taught in small groups with a great deal of nurturing interaction between the teacher and the student and between each student and his or her peers (Hale, 2001).

- *Diminish the use of photocopied worksheets, workbooks, textbooks, and a "skill-and-drill" orientation.* Emphasis should be placed on hands-on activities, projects, interrelated learning experiences, field trips, speakers, and classroom visitors.

- *Provide cultural-enrichment activities.* Cultural-enrichment activities are extremely important for African American students. In the past, the interactions within large extended families served as vehicles for socialization, providing students with the social skills and moral training needed for the development of positive character traits (Hale, 1986).

- *Utilize looping.* Keeping students with the same teacher(s) for two years or more can promote increased achievement because relationships are strengthened.

- *Blend of the creative arts.* Given the immersion in the creative arts in most African American households, the infusion of this will increase the interest in activities and stimulate motivation to achieve (Hale, 1986).

- *Provide culturally relevant instructional material.* In an effort to make the curriculum more culturally relevant, it is imperative to provide among instructional materials, core content texts, literature, and arts materials that are by and about African Americans. This includes historical descriptions of African Americans who have made significant contributions to this country and the world (Ladson-Billings, 1994).

- *Maintain high expectations for all children*. Harboring low expectations for students, especially students that are living in poverty or that are culturally or linguistically diverse, is debilitating because it conveys to students a sense that they are inadequate. Furthermore, once students internalize this belief, feelings of inferiority abound, and students are more likely to view themselves as self-fulfilling prophecies.

to care that he is making failing grades. She has tried some strategies to address this problem, including giving tangible incentives for improved work and offering to stay after school to work individually with him. The incentives proved unsuccessful; Manual has shown no improvement in his school work, and has not stayed after school. Manuel currently receives three hours per week of ESOL services.

Mrs. Lovett has noticed that, although Manuel speaks English quite well, he doesn't engage in discussions or answer questions in class. She is unsure if this is more evidence of his growing lack of motivation or if it is related to his language acquisition. Mrs. Lovett has tested Manuel's reading fluency using the DIBELS. His oral reading fluency score in September was 112 words per minute. The benchmark score for students at the end of third grade is 110 words per minute. Although Manuel has achieved the benchmark, he is considered to have achieved the minimum standard for reading fluency. Manuel's retell fluency (reading comprehension) score was eleven. This score indicates that Manuel was able to retell only 10% of what he read. An acceptable score for retell fluency would be at least 25% of the passage-relevant words. Mrs. Lovett feels she needs assistance from her school's Student Support Team, which is a building-level assistance team that assists teachers in working to increase student achievement.

The school's building-level team is composed of a curriculum coordinator who also serves as facilitator for the team, the school's literacy coach, and the math coach. Other members are added as needed based on the problems each referred student is experiencing. For Manuel's team, the ESOL teacher, school counselor, and a fourth-grade teacher are added to the team. This team will meet with Mrs. Lovett on an ongoing basis to explore the causes of Manuel's difficulties and provide guidance for addressing these problems.

At the first meeting, team members discuss Manuel's educational history based on the records available to them. They find that Manuel entered second grade two years earlier in September. At the time, he knew some conversational English. Manuel was placed in a general education second-grade class and was provided ESOL services for three hours each week by the itinerant ESOL teacher. Manuel was assigned to a peer helper who was also an English language learner, but who had been in the school for over a year. Other accommodations at the time included reduced amount of work, extra time for completion of tasks, and small-group work for additional help in reading and math. It was noted in his records that Manuel progressed rapidly in English language acquisition. His records indicated that, although Manuel's parents spoke very little English, his family lived with his aunt, who had lived in the United States for several years and was fluent in English. It was also noted that she often assisted Manuel with his homework.

After discussing these issues, the team recommends sending home a background information form to learn more about Manuel's functioning outside of school and his academic history prior to coming to Park Street School. They request a meeting with Manuel's parents to discuss these issues as well. It is noted that Manuel's parents were invited to the earlier team meeting, but did not respond to the invitation. Mrs. Garcia, the ESOL teacher, will contact them by phone and encourage them to meet with the team.

Mrs. Garcia also discusses with the team the differences between conversational and academic English. Manuel's English proficiency was assessed in February using an assessment tool called "Assessing Comprehension and Communication in English State to State for English Language Learners" (ACCESS for ELLs™). ACCESS for ELLs™, a language proficiency test for K–12 students, is the standardized language-assessment tool used by several states to determine language proficiency and eligibility for ESOL services. On the ACCESS for ELLs™, Manuel scored a standard score of 420 in comprehension. His composite score yielded a language proficiency level of 3.4, which places Manuel at the developing level. Students functioning at this level have general and some specific language of the content areas, but some difficulty with specific academic language (Gottlieb, 2006).

The team decides to implement a Tier One intervention to address Manuel's reading comprehension deficit. The team chooses to implement a research-based strategy called Peer-Assisted Learning Strategies (PALS). PALS has been empirically tested for its effectiveness with English language learners and has been found to significantly improve reading comprehension for ELLs who are also learning disabled (Saenz et al., 2005). Mrs. Lovett will implement the strategy during supplemental reading instruction for thirty minutes per day, four days per week. The strategy is planned for implementation over eight weeks. Mrs. Lovett also chooses to increase the frequency of progress monitoring to twice per week, using the DIBELS retell fluency assessment.

Manuel's progress during the eight weeks of intervention is illustrated in Figure 4.1. Although his oral reading fluency score has improved only slightly to 118 words per minute, his retell fluency has increased to twenty-four. It is apparent that Manuel's reading comprehension is showing considerable improvement with the intervention. Mrs. Lovett also notes that Manuel is completing more assignments in class and displays a more positive attitude than prior to the intervention.

Manuel's parents, Mr. and Mrs. Rodriguez, attend the next team meeting. Mrs. Garcia acts as an interpreter during the meeting. Mrs. Lovett presents the results of the PALS intervention. Mr. Rodriguez reports that

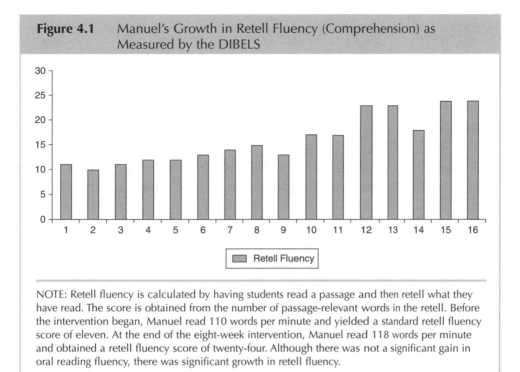

Figure 4.1 Manuel's Growth in Retell Fluency (Comprehension) as Measured by the DIBELS

NOTE: Retell fluency is calculated by having students read a passage and then retell what they have read. The score is obtained from the number of passage-relevant words in the retell. Before the intervention began, Manuel read 110 words per minute and yielded a standard retell fluency score of eleven. At the end of the eight-week intervention, Manuel read 118 words per minute and obtained a retell fluency score of twenty-four. Although there was not a significant gain in oral reading fluency, there was significant growth in retell fluency.

Manuel attended first grade in Mexico City. He reportedly had no problems in school, but official records are unavailable. Manuel's family life in Mexico was stable with no significant problems. Manuel has no history of significant illnesses or injuries. Mr. and Mrs. Rodriguez speak Spanish at home, but Mr. Rodriguez speaks some English. Manuel's aunt speaks fluent English, as reported earlier. Manuel stays with his aunt after school each day.

After discussing these issues and Manuel's progress with the PALS intervention, the team decides to continue the Tier One intervention for an additional eight-week period. Data indicates that Manuel's English language proficiency continues to be low, possibly causing many of the problems Manuel is experiencing. Mrs. Garcia provides additional suggestions regarding strategies to improve Manuel's success in class.

The decision to continue with the Tier One strategy was based on Manuel's English language proficiency, his positive response to the intervention, and the absence of significant external factors. If Manuel had not exhibited a positive response to the intervention, the team would have needed to determine if a new strategy was needed as a Tier Two intervention.

CONCLUSION

Although RTI is a new process in determining eligibility, many factors affect educational attainment. Thus, many factors also affect one's interpretation of a response to any intervention among students that are culturally and linguistically diverse. Teasing out the impact of these factors on the RTI process will require research on actual implementation of RTI with students from diverse groups, which has yet to be conducted. Nevertheless, as teachers move into the RTI process, almost all will confront questions on how that process specifically impacts every student, and consideration of this issue will be critical in every eligibility case.

REFERENCES

Apiwattanalunggarn, K. L., & Luster, T. (2005). Individual differences in the school performance of 2nd-grade children born to low-income adolescent mothers: Findings from an 8-year longitudinal study. *Journal of Research in Childhood Education, 19*(4), 314–332.

Batsche, G., Elliott, J., Graden, J. L., Grimes, J., Kovaleski, J. E., & Prasse, D. et al. (2006). *Response to intervention: Policy considerations and implementation.* Alexandra, VA: National Association of State Directors of Special Education.

Carrasquillo, A. L., & Rodriguez, J. (1997). Hispanic limited English-proficient students with disabilities. *Learning Disabilities: A Multidisciplinary Journal, 8*(3), 167–174.

Council for Exceptional Children. (2002). *Addressing over-representation of African American students in special education: The prereferral intervention process—An administrator's guide.* Washington, DC: National Alliance of Black School Educators.

Cummins, J. (1979). Linguistic interdependence and the educational development of bilingual children. *Review of Educational Research, 49,* 222–251.

Cummins, J. (1980). The entry and exit fallacy in bilingual education. *NABE Journal, 4*(3), 25–29.

Darling-Hammond, L. (Ed.). (1994). Assessment and diversity. *Review of Research in Education, 20,* 337–391.

Donovan, M. S., & Cross, C. T. (2002). *Minority students in special and gifted education.* Washington, DC: National Research Council.

Ellison, C. M., Boykin, A. W., Towns, D. P., & Stokes, A. (2000). *Classroom cultural ecology: The dynamics of classroom life in schools serving low-income African American children.* Washington, DC: Howard University, Center for Research on the Education of Students Placed at Risk.

Fierros, E. G., & Conroy, J. W. (2002). Double jeopardy: An exploration of restrictiveness and race in special education. In D. J. Losen & G. Orfield (Eds.), *Racial inequity in special education* (pp. 39–70). Cambridge, MA: Harvard Educational Press.

Fletcher, J. M., Shaywitz, S. E., Shankweiler, D. P., Katz, L., Lieberman, I. Y., Stuebing, K. K., et al. (1994). Cognitive profiles of reading disability: Comparisons of discrepancy and low achievement definitions. *Journal of Educational Psychology, 86,* 6–23.

Forman, E. G., & Conroy, J. W. (1992). Changing perspectives in writing instruction. *The Reading Teacher, 35,* 550–556.

Freeman, D., & Freeman, Y. (2004). Three types of English language learners. *School Talk: Newsletter of the National Council of Teachers of English,* 9(4), 1–3.

Garcia, G. E., & Pearson, P. D. (1994). Assessment and diversity. In L. Darling-Hammond (Ed.), *Review of research in education, 20,* (pp. 337–391). Washington, DC: American Educational Research Association.

Gottlieb, M. (2006, Spring). *Interpretive guide for score reports.* Retrieved August 30, 2006, from http://public.doe.k12.ga.us

Grossman, H. (1985). *Special education in a diverse society.* Boston, MA: Allyn & Bacon.

Hale, J. E. (1986). *Black children: Their roots, culture, and learning styles.* Baltimore, MD: Johns Hopkins University Press.

Hale, J. E. (2001). Learning while black: Creating educational excellence for African American children. Baltimore, MD: John Hopkins University Press.

Hodgkinson, H. (1995). What should we call people? Race, class, and the census for 2000. *Phi Delta Kappan, 77,* 173–179.

Hosp, J. L., & Reschly, D. J. (2004). Disproportionate representation of minority students in special education: Academic, demographic, and economic predictors. *Exceptional Children, 70*(2), 185–199.

Ishii-Jordan, S. R. (1997). When behavior differences are not disorders. In A. J. Artiles & G. Zamora-Duran (Eds.), *Reducing disproportionate representation of culturally diverse students in special and gifted education* (pp. 27–46). Reston, VA: Council for Exceptional Children.

Klingner, J. K., & Artiles, A. J. (2003). When should bilingual students be in special education? *Educational Leadership, 61*(2), 66–71.

Kunjufu, J. (2002). *Black student, middle class teachers.* Chicago, Illinois: African-American Images.

Ladson-Billings, G. (1994). *The dreamkeepers: Successful teachers of African American children.* San Francisco, CA: Josey-Bass.

Lindsey, K. A., Manis, F. R., & Bailey, C. E. (2003). Prediction of first-grade reading in Spanish-speaking English-language learners. *Journal of Educational Psychology, 95*(3), 482–494.

Marler, B., & Sanchez-Lopez, C. (2006, April). *Distinguishing learning disabilities from academic difficulties for English language learners.* Presentation at the 2006 Council for Exceptional Children's Conference, Salt Lake City, UT.

National Center for Culturally Responsive Educational Systems. (2005, Fall). *Cultural considerations and challenges in response-to-intervention models.* Retrieved September 15, 2006, from www.nccrest.org/publication/position_statements/html

National Center for Culturally Responsive Educational Systems. (2006). *Preventing disproportionality by strengthening district policies and procedures: An assessment and strategic planning process.* Retrieved August 3, 2006, from http://www.nccrest.org/index.html

National Council for Teachers of English. (2006, April). *NCTE position paper on the role of English teachers in educating English language learners.* Retrieved September 2, 2006, from www.ncte.org

National Institute for Urban School Improvement. (2001). *On the nexus of race, disability and overrepresentation: What do we know? Where do we go?* Washington, DC: Office of Special Education Programs, U. S. Department of Education.

Ochoa, S. H., Rivera, B. D., & Powell, M. P. (1997). Factors used to comply with the exclusionary clause with bilingual and limited-English-proficient pupils: Initial guidelines. *Learning Disabilities Research & Practice, 12,* 161–167.

Oswald, D. P., Coutinho, M. J., Best, A. M., & Nguyen, N. (2001). Impact of sociodemographic characteristics on the identification rates of minority students as having mental retardation. *Mental Retardation, 39*(5), 351–367.

Paolino, A. (2003). *Addressing disproportionality of minority students in special education programs.* Retrieved August 30, 2006, from http://www.ecs.org/html

Payne, R. K. (2005). *A framework for understanding poverty.* Highlands, TX: aha! Process, Inc.

President's Commission on Excellence in Special Education. (2002). *A new era: Revitalizing special education for children and their families.* Retrieved July 26, 2006, from www.ed.gov/inits/commissionsboards/index.html.

Reschly, D. J., & Hosp, J. L. (2004). State SLD identification policies and practices. *Learning Disability Quarterly, 27*(4), 197–213.

Saenz, L. M., Fuchs, L. S., & Fuchs, D. (2005). Peer-assisted learning strategies for English language learners with learning disabilities. *Exceptional Children, 71*(3), 231–247.

Scruggs, T. E., & Mastriopieri, M. A. (2002). On babies and bathwater: Addressing the problems of identification of learning disabilities. *Learning Disability Quarterly, 25*(3), 155–164.

Sousa, D. A. (2006). *How the brain learns* (3rd Ed., pp. 165–212). Thousand Oaks, CA: Corwin Press.

Stanovich, K. E. (1999). The sociopsychometrics of learning disabilities. *Journal of Learning Disabilities, 32,* 350–361.

Strickland, D. S. (1994). Educating African American learners at risk: Finding a better way. *Language Arts, 71*(5), 328–336.

Tomlinson, C. (1999). *The differentiated classroom: Responding to the needs of all learners.* Alexandria, VA: Association for Supervision and Curriculum Development.

Toppo, G. (2000, September 3). Wages rise, but families work more: Blacks, Hispanics put in longer hours than white counterparts to earn same. *Detroit News,* 17A.

U.S. Census Bureau. (2003a, October). *Language use and English speaking ability: 2000.* Washington, DC: U.S. Government Printing Office.

U.S. Census Bureau. (2003b, February 25). *U.S. Census Bureau, population division.* Retrieved June 2006, from www.ed.gov/population

U.S. Census Bureau. (2006, August 29). *Annual demographic survey: March supplement.* Retrieved September 15, 2006, from http://pubdb3.census.gov

U. S. Department of Education. (2002). *Twenty-fourth annual report to Congress on the implementation of the Individuals with Disabilities Education Act.* Retrieved August 30, 2006, from http://www.ed.gov

U.S. Office of Education. (2006). *Federal Regulations on IDEA of 2004.* Retrieved November 29, 2006, from http://IDEA.ed.gov/explore/view/p/, root, regs, 300,D,300%252E309

Valdez, G., & Figueroa, R. A. (1994). *Bilingualism and testing: A special case of bias.* Norwood, NJ: Ablex.

Vaughn, S., & Fuchs, L. S. (2003). Redefining learning disabilities as inadequate response to instruction: The promise and potential problems. *Learning Disabilities Research & Practice, 18*(3), 137–146.

Vaughn, S., Linan-Thompson, S., Mathes, P. G., Cirino, P. T., Carlson, C. D., & Pollard-Durodola, S. D. et al. (2006). Effectiveness of Spanish intervention for first-grade English language learners at risk for reading difficulties. *Journal of Learning Disabilities, 39*(1), 56–73.

Vaughn, S., Mathes, P. G., Linan-Thompson, S., & Francis, D. J. (2005). Teaching English language learners at risk for reading disabilities to read: Putting research into practice. *Learning Disabilities Research & Practice, 20*(1), 58–67.

Vellutino, F. R., Scanlon, D. M., Small, S., & Fanuele, D. P. (2006). Response to intervention as a vehicle for distinguishing between children with and without reading disabilities: Evidence for the role of kindergarten and first-grade interventions. *Journal of Learning Disabilities, 39*(2), 157–169.

5 Will RTI Work?

Ongoing Questions

William N. Bender, Lisa Ulmer,
Michael R. Baskette, and Cara Shores

S ince the recent passage of the 2004 Reauthorization of IDEA, many researchers and practitioners have heard of the proposed change to use RTI to document eligibility of students for learning disabilities. Not all questions have been answered, however, concerning implementation of this procedure (Gersten & Dimino, 2006; Kavale, Holdnack, & Mostert, 2006). Although not a new concept by any means, RTI is nevertheless somewhat "untried" as an eligibility tool (Kavale et al., 2006). Further, the available literature indicates that various authors have applied RTI in different ways for students with disabilities (Marston, 2005; O'Conner, 2003; Vaughn, 2003), and even the most basic questions seemingly remain unanswered. These include the following:

- Will the implementation of RTI decrease or increase the prevalence of students with LD?
- How can we tell the difference between a student with a learning disability and a low achieving student?
- Should RTI be the sole criterion for identification of a learning disability?
- Is RTI new?
- What is the relationship between the non–special education interventions in Tiers One and Two and special education instruction?
- How do educators best specify appropriate Responsiveness to Intervention
- Does the LD status of some students change with implementation of RTI?

- What happens to students who are gifted and have LD?
- What happens to students who are nonverbal and have LD?
- What happens to students who are "slow learners?"
- Will all students currently served as LD be eligible under RTI?

These and many other questions remain unanswered; the purpose of this chapter is, at a minimum, to present these questions, and, where possible, suggest viable solutions.

WILL RTI DECREASE THE PREVALENCE OF LD?

Since the introduction of learning disability (LD) in the Education for All Handicapped Children Act (PL 94-142, 1975), there has been much debate over the accuracy of the LD prevalence rate. Further, the population of individuals identified with LD has increased by 150%–200% since its introduction in 1975 (Bradley, Danielson, Doolittle, 2005; Wagner & Garon, 1999; U.S. Department of Education, 2000), and prevalence figures now seem to hover between 2%–8%. Based on this drastic increase, Wong (1996) suggested that teachers may have included all students with learning difficulties under the label of LD and not limited the LD diagnosis at all. When considering implementation of RTI, one question we should ask is: Will the implementation of RTI decrease or increase the prevalence of LD?

Reflection 5.1	Have You Participated?

Many educators in the field have been concerned with the ever-increasing number of students with learning disabilities over the years. However, when we wonder where the increasing prevalence rates among students with LD come from, it may be worthwhile to examine our own actions. We have participated in eligibility meetings in which students with an IQ lower than eighty-five were being considered for services as LD; if we believed that placement in the LD resource or inclusion programs would benefit these children, we have "signed off" on such placements, while knowing this action was questionable. Of course, we participated in those decisions for a very worthy reason—we believed that such placements would benefit the children; no professional should apologize for making decisions on that basis. With that stated, such determinations to place students in LD classes who may not exactly meet all of the criteria does take up needed resources, and lead to increasing LD prevalence rates. In short, although many factors may affect the increasing prevalence rates, we feel we need look no further than ourselves to find out where some of the problems may lie. Thus, we invite each reader to consider his or her ethical responsibility in this regard.

In all of the discussions of prevalence, there appear to be three issues that affect the prevalence rate of LD: variability in prevalence rates, conceptual problems in definitions of LD, and specificity of the LD construct. Each of these issues is discussed here.

Variability in Prevalence Rates

Although prevalence rates vary from study to study, recall from Chapter 1 that the accepted prevalence rates of students with LD range from a low of 2.96% in Kentucky to a high of 9.46% in Rhode Island (Coutinho, 1995; Finlan, 1992; Reshley, Hosp, & Schmied, 2003). Of course, this variability in prevalence rates from state to state would seem to indicate either a substantial difference in the size of the LD population overall or vastly different eligibility standards for LD from one state to another. Some have proposed that the implementation of RTI would decrease some of the variability in prevalence rates, because RTI is based on scientifically validated educational curricula. As this perspective goes, regardless of the state, students who are challenged by academic work will be presented with data-based instruction and their response will determine eligibility. Thus, this RTI procedure, once implemented in every state, should stabilize the prevalence rate for LD and decrease the size of the population identified as learning disabled.

However, this set of propositions is not at all certain. First, such RTI protocols have not been widely utilized as eligibility tools; practitioners in the field cannot be certain how implementation of this concept will affect prevalence rates (Gersten & Dimino, 2006; Kavale et al., 2006). Next, we must note a phenomenon that has not to our knowledge been discussed previously in the RTI literature—the age of onset of LD. For the last several decades, the bulk of students identified as learning disabled have been so identified at some point during their third-or fourth-grade year; thus, the age of onset for LD seems to be around the age of nine or ten. In fact, teachers in the recent past seemed to wish to "give the benefit of doubt" to students struggling with academic work in kindergarten, Grade 1, or Grade 2. However, under the RTI model, and given the emphasis of all of the available literature on phonologically based early-reading problems, one may well assume that students who do not perform well on phonological exercises in kindergarten, or "Rapid Letter Naming" tests or word-mastery exercises in Grades 1 and 2 might now be identified as learning disabled. In short, in the recent past, we've been identifying students in only the last ten years of their thirteen-year public school career. Under RTI, such identification is much more likely in all thirteen of these public school years. This fact alone may increase the prevalence of LD. Some studies that have used RTI as a way of determining eligibility have shown prevalence rates for learning disabilities that are at least as high or higher than current rates (O'Conner, 2003; Vaughn, 2003); other studies, however, show no change in prevalence rates (Marston, Muyskens, Lau, & Canter, 2003). Still, at present we simply don't know if RTI is likely to reduce prevalence of LD, particularly when we consider the traditional age of onset for LD and changes that might occur in that age, once RTI is implemented.

Conceptual Problems in Definitions of LD

Probably the principal cause for the high variability of prevalence rates among states is the absence of a standard definition of learning disability (Kavale & Forness, 2000). In fact, many state definitions differ considerably from one another. Thus, a student may manifest a disability in one state and not in another which, in turn, can lead to differing prevalence rates among the states. Presumably, using the RTI model, this variability would be eliminated because students who fail to respond to interventions in one state would likely fail to respond in another.

However, given the wide variety of educational interventions that could be utilized in the RTI procedure, it might be possible for higher variability in prevalence rates to result. For example, some states might exclusively delineate phonologically based reading interventions as the only acceptable intervention for RTI utilization, whereas other states might allow the use of any scientifically validated curriculum in any subject area (e.g., a direct-instructional program in mathematics or language arts, or perhaps even a scientifically validated, computerized social studies curriculum). Thus, this utilization of a wider range of acceptable curriculum could possibly result in a higher prevalence of LD in that state. Thus, it is not certain that shifting to an RTI procedure will reduce interstate variability in prevalence rates.

Specificity of the LD Construct

The specificity issue addresses the question: How can we tell the difference between students with learning disability and low-achieving students? Many researchers have suggested that individuals with learning disability cannot be reliably distinguished from individuals with low achievement. Others have stated more specifically that students with reading disabilities cannot be distinguished from generally poor readers (Algozzine, 1985; Fletcher & Foorman, 1994; Fletcher, Francis, Rourke, & Shaywitz, 1992; Spear-Swerling, 1999; Wagner & Garon, 1999; Ysseldyke, Algozzine, Shinn, & McGue, 1982). In one early study comparing low achievers to students identified with learning disabilities, Ysseldyke, Algozzine, Richey, and Graden (1982) concluded that the two groups were psychometrically equivalent. These results highlight one of the long-standing issues in learning disabilities—specificity of the learning disabilities construct. How do we know when a student has LD?

Proponents of RTI argue that implementation of RTI could assist in eliminating some of the specificity concerns, because RTI would probably allow the teacher to distinguish between a student with a learning disability and a student who is low achieving. Students who respond to the intensive interventions in Tiers One and Two would presumably be low achieving for some reason other than a learning disability. Thus, in this one area, RTI seems to hold the promise for addressing one of the longest-standing concerns in the field of learning disabilities.

However, this has yet to be established by research, and some research indicates that this assumption may be wishful thinking. In one early study, RTI was shown to reduce the number of culturally and linguistically diverse students referred to special education (Marsten et al., 2003). Yet in the same report, the authors noted that RTI was prone to systematic errors in identifying students with LD. Specifically, those errors arose from the potential for RTI to identify students who are generally low achievers, such as students who are poor and culturally and linguistically diverse. In point of fact, it has not been established that RTI will reliably discriminate between students with learning disabilities and students with other learning challenges.

SHOULD RTI BE THE SOLE CRITERION FOR LEARNING DISABILITY?

Scruggs and Mastropieri (2002) suggested that any alternative to the current diagnostic procedures must include certain criteria that are considered to be valid and that are met with general acceptance. These criteria include the following (Scruggs & Mastropieri, 2002):

- The procedures must address the multifaceted nature of a learning disability.
- The procedures must be able to be administered across the age spectrum.
- Administrators of the procedures must be able to demonstrate technical adequacy of the procedures.
- The procedures must show a reduction in overidentification of LD.
- The procedures must reduce inappropriate variability across state and local agencies.
- The procedures must identify students that meet the conceptualizations of learning disability.

Given the previous discussion, it is at least plausible that RTI will fail to meet one or more of these criteria. Thus, as a field, we may wish to consider implementation of RTI in combination with other procedures. In fact, one alternative to exclusive use of RTI is implementation of RTI in combination with the current discrepancy criteria (Scruggs & Mastropieri, 2002). Thus, both discrepancy procedures and the RTI model would be used; the discrepancy criteria to document discrepancy and normal levels of intelligence and the RTI to distinguish between the students responding and the students not responding to research-based interventions.

Under this proposal, when it is determined that the child is not responding to interventions, both psychological/IQ and achievement tests would be administered to the child to determine if a discrepancy exists. If a discrepancy exists at a predetermined level, the information on the child would then be submitted to a referral team to decide on placement and setting issues. If a student does not have the predetermined discrepancy, then there should be some form of support for the student other than services as learning disabled (Scruggs & Mastropieri , 2002).

Initially, this combination approach has some appeal. One strength of this dual model for diagnosis is the fact that valid, evidence-based instruction is provided to all students before any eligibility determination is made. This ensures that students are given sound instruction. This also ensures that any lack of achievement is due to a disability within the student and not as a result of the instructional procedures. Although it is hoped by professionals, as well as mandated by law, that every student be given good instruction, the fact is that there is no federal or state system in place that we are aware of that allows for documentation of "effective instruction." Thus, any procedure that facilitates improved instruction holds some appeal for concerned professionals.

Another strength of this dual approach involves the distinction between students with a learning disability and "slow learners" who may have a lower than average IQ. Presumably more students with an IQ in the range of seventy to eighty-five would be somewhat less responsive to instruction than students with an IQ of over eighty-five; coupling RTI with the discrepancy procedures currently in place would prevent those students with the lower IQ from becoming labeled as learning disabled.

Some estimates of the "slow learner" population suggest that around 15% of the total population may be slower learners (Scruggs & Mastropieri, 2002), and this is almost twice the rate of LD prevalence of even the highest prevalence states currently. Clearly, if that group were allowed to "drain" resources intended for students with learning disabilities, school districts nationwide would have serious concerns. Many students with lower IQs would not respond to instruction, and therefore could conceivably drain the federal and state budgets for students with learning disabilities. However, it is uncertain how the RTI procedure, when utilized alone, would deal with the "slow learners."

Although taking positions on which eligibility considerations should be utilized is always fraught with danger, we will state our opinion. We believe that discrepancy calculations have outlived their usefulness and should be discontinued in favor of RTI procedures as described in Chapters 2 and 3. We feel that this offers the best, most efficient approach for determining eligibility of students suspected of having a learning disability. Also, the implementation of RTI promises enhanced instruction for all students in the class, as all teachers become more familiar with this best-teaching practice. For this reason, teachers are likely to become better equipped to deal with the learning needs of slower learners in the class, as well as students with learning disabilities.

IS RTI NEW?

Although the Response to Instruction idea has received a great deal of attention since the report of the Presidential Commission on Excellence in Special Education (2002), only in December 2004 was the legislation passed that allowed the use of RTI as an eligibility procedure (Marston et al., 2003). Further, the final rules and regulations related to RTI became official as recently as August 2006. Still, we might well ask, is RTI really a new idea or a new version of an old requirement? Gersten and Dimino (2006) discussed the apparent similarity between RTI procedures and the prereferral interventions that have been required since the late 1980s for all students with special needs. As these authors indicate, prereferral interventions have proven to be significant challenges to many general education teachers. In Chapter 3, we discussed Flugum and Reschly's (1994) study of the quality of prereferral interventions in Heartland Area Educational Agency's schools. According to their study, teams were providing few interventions and the ones provided were of poor quality. We also discussed a report on the Minneapolis Public School's problem-solving model, in which the evaluators stated that data on student progress was inconsistent (Deno, Grimes, Reschly, & Schrag, 2001).

As practitioners in the field of learning disabilities, we have personally encountered these same problems in our experiences with problem-solving teams. We have seen school-based eligibility teams who seem to "talk the talk," but who don't "walk the walk" when it comes to actually implementing prereferral interventions with rigor. This may suggest that, although teachers in our nation have become skilled at planning prereferral

interventions, they are less proficient at actually implementing such interventions and monitoring a student's progress.

Thus, even with this new legislation in place, are teachers trained
to implement Tier One and Two interventions and will they monitor
students' progress with rigor? The answer to this question is not certain,
but we would suggest that in the recent past, implementation of prereferral interventions and behavioral-improvement plans has been less
than adequate in many cases. Certainly, school systems must take every
step necessary to provide teachers with the skills to fully implement the
RTI process.

In a related question, will the Tier One interventions (previously
described as the first step in the RTI procedure) replace the current requirement for prereferral interventions for students suspected of demonstrating
a learning disability, since both of these interventions take place in the
general education classroom? We have heard some school administrators
indicate "yes" and others indicate "no" to that question. One school administrator even suggested the possibility of using current state and/or
federal programs in reading instruction (e.g., Title One programs, as one
example), as the Tier One intervention in the RTI process. Does this suggest that every student who does not progress in a Title One program may
be considered for a learning disability? Of course, placement of students in
certain federally funded programs may not be appropriate because those
programs may be limited to particular groups of students. Still, to date,
the question of how RTI relates to prereferral services is an unanswered
question.

WHAT IS THE RELATIONSHIP BETWEEN NON–SPECIAL EDUCATION INTERVENTIONS IN TIERS ONE AND TWO AND SPECIAL EDUCATION INSTRUCTION?

What is the relationship between non–special education interventions in
Tiers One and Two and special education instruction? Although this question has not as yet been answered in the field, we can suggest one possible
answer. Historically, special education has been reluctant to utilize existing
procedures for documentation of the need for special services. As one
example, special education has not generally recognized the use of group-
administered assessment scores in eligibility determinations, but, rather,
has insisted on individually administered assessments for documentation
of eligibility decisions. Following that general principle in moving toward
implementation of RTI, perhaps we should require teachers to implement

rigorous instruction using scientifically validated instructional procedures and also prohibit the use of instructional data that is routinely generated in the general education class in the RTI process. Such a requirement might lead to more effective implementation of scientifically validated instruction for many students, because such a requirement would probably result in various in-service instructional opportunities on RTI for many teachers. Teachers in general education would then be somewhat better prepared to implement RTI practices for many students in the class.

However, multiple educational interventions may well prove too costly—in either time or money—so our recommendation is that interventions that are routinely conducted in the general education or federally funded basic skills programs be used when appropriate as Tier One interventions, but not as Tier Two interventions. We believe that Tier Two interventions should be exclusively related to the child in question. Thus, we hope to encourage the teacher to concentrate on the instructional and eligibility issues at hand and to implement the intervention with integrity and instructional validity.

In earlier chapters (see Table 2.3), we recommended use of federal reading interventions programs as Tier One interventions. This seems to be a possibility under present guidelines, and we feel that use of data from such interventions in Tier One is quite appropriate, contingent on two important criteria:

1. The intervention must be targeted to the specific learning needs of the target student, and

2. The intervention must result in appropriate data for decision-making purposes.

If a student's reading problem is based on reading fluency deficits and low vocabulary scores, and not on phonological deficits, a Tier One reading intervention in a Title One reading program that focused on phonological skills would probably not be considered as an appropriate Tier One intervention for that child. However, the same Title One reading program would be very appropriate as a Tier One intervention for a student whose reading problems in the general education class were related to phonological deficits. Again, as long as the Tier One intervention is directly related to the specific academic problems demonstrated by the target child, it would be considered an appropriate Tier One intervention. Of course, all Tier One interventions must result in appropriate curriculum-based measurement data on a daily, biweekly, or weekly basis, because the RTI process is dependent on the generation of highly specific data that represents a child's learning profile over time.

HOW DO EDUCATORS BEST SPECIFY APPROPRIATE RESPONSIVENESS TO INTERVENTION?

One of the many unanswered questions regarding RTI is how to best determine the appropriate level of Responsiveness to Intervention. In short, how much learning is considered adequate progress for a particular child? This question has been addressed by various researchers, but there is no agreement on what distinguishes responders from nonresponders, in the RTI process.

Fuchs and his coworkers (Fuchs & Fuchs, 2005, 2006; Fuchs, Fuchs, & Compton, 2004) suggested using the twenty-fifth percentile as a cutpoint for placement in Tier One. Adequate response for Tiers Two and Three was suggested as scoring above the sixteenth percentile. Various other researchers have used one standard deviation as the cutpoint. We recommend that districts consider 20% as an appropriate cutpoint for all interventions; we believe this cutpoint will capture the students who need an RTI process. Also, we think simplicity is essential whenever possible during the RTI process; therefore, we do not suggest differential cutpoints for the different tiers.

One possible solution for determining the appropriate level of responsiveness is to use a teaching method that has cutpoints programmed into the process. Precision Teaching (PT) is one such method. Precision Teaching has been used to facilitate progress for a wide range of learners from those with severe handicaps to graduate students (White, 1985). It can provide the teacher with a quick, yet constant and precise measure of the skill acquisition of each child. Precision Teaching allows learning to be measured through the systematic use of recording devices, such as daily charts, on which student responses are plotted (White, 1985). Probes or task sheets are used to monitor target skills daily. Unlike standardized tests, which only test a small sample of skills, PT provides a direct measure of performance by using frequency of response to measure the number of correct and incorrect responses in a specific time period (typically a one-minute period).

For example, Figures 5.1 and 5.2 show data collected over a thirty-day period in a middle school math class in which PT was implemented. Daily one-minute probes were used for two-digit by two-digit and two-digit by three-digit multiplication problems. Each day, the student, Anthony, received ten minutes of direct instruction before completing his ten-question probe. Using the median of the class scores for each probe sheet (ten correct responses), the teacher could quickly set goals for Anthony.

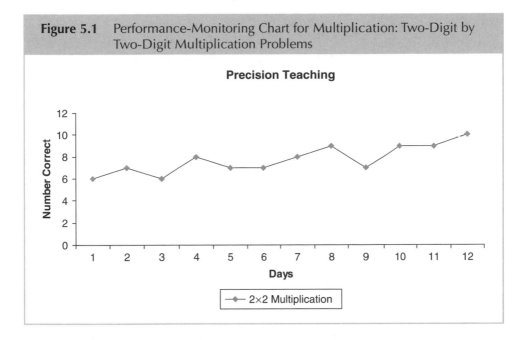

Figure 5.1   Performance-Monitoring Chart for Multiplication: Two-Digit by Two-Digit Multiplication Problems

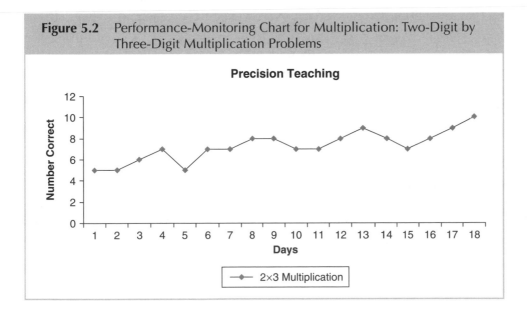

Figure 5.2   Performance-Monitoring Chart for Multiplication: Two-Digit by Three-Digit Multiplication Problems

On Day 1 of implementation of two-digit by two-digit multiplication problems, he scored six correct responses. On Day 12 of intervention, he scored ten correct responses in a one-minute period. On Day 13, two-digit by three-digit multiplication was introduced; Anthony scored five correct responses. Seventeen days later, his number of correct responses increased to nine correct responses per minute. The acceleration shown on the chart indicates that Anthony's number of correct responses increased over a period of thirty days. Thus, he responded to intervention and reached the average level of achievement consistent with the achievement of his peers.

There is an additional advantage of using PT as a model for RTI. To date, the majority of research done on RTI is limited to reading intervention studies done with children in Grades K–3. There are limited data available to indicate the effects of using RTI with math or using it in reading intervention with students beyond Grade 3. In the field, however, educators may face the necessity, at least on occasion, to document RTI for students in higher grades. Specifically, students in middle school and high school also have difficulties with basic reading and math skills and need to be identified in order to receive services/intervention. RTI interventions must not be limited to those that are geared towards early intervention. RTI interventions must include methods such as PT that can work at any age, any level, and with varying types of disabilities, so that secondary students and students with disabilities in mathematics, language arts, and/or other subjects are not overlooked.

As an example, one of the authors used PT methods in a ninth-grade World History inclusion classroom. Melissa was given multiple choice/matching tests at the end of each chapter. Teaching probes that presented factual questions from the class were used with each unit (e.g., River Civilizations, Ancient Egypt) to help students break down information into chunks and commit it to memory. The probe sheet, which all the students completed each day, consisted of sixteen blocks on the front with fill-in-the-blank questions in each block. Sixteen blank corresponding blocks were placed on the back of the sheet so students could write the answers from the questions on the front of the sheet. Students were then given blank probes throughout the week and a one-minute period to see how many they could answer correctly.

Data for Melissa were collected and charted, because Melissa had demonstrated difficulties in previous grades. As the data in Figure 5.3 shows, the PT probes were highly effective; Melissa's chart showed considerable growth in this secondary subject area. These Tier One data demonstrate that Melissa could profit from effective instruction in secondary social studies. Overall, in this particular class, over 90% of students with and without disabilities correctly answered the multiple-choice questions from the probe sheets on their unit test. Thus, these data indicate that such PT-based instruction could serve as an effective Tier One intervention.

We should point out that the implementation of Precision Teaching principles has been a growing phenomenon in special education, although the term "Precision Teaching" has not been widely utilized recently. Many of the principles of Precision Teaching are currently embodied in curriculum-based measurement procedures which, over the last thirty years, have been widely studied (Deno, 2003).

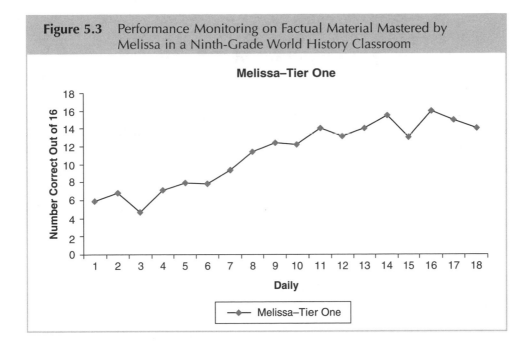

Figure 5.3 Performance Monitoring on Factual Material Mastered by Melissa in a Ninth-Grade World History Classroom

Research has documented the technical adequacy of this type of progress monitoring, as well as the efficiency of curriculum-based measurements for classroom settings (Deno, 2003; Fuchs & Fuchs, 2005). Further, curriculum-based measurement has been employed as both a screening tool—to identify students who may require special assistance—and a prereferral intervention procedure. For purposes of RTI implementation, we believe that Precision Teaching methods, as embodied in the current emphasis on curriculum-based measurement, will be the best option for appropriately monitoring pupil response to interventions.

Reflection 5.2 How Responsive Can Our Instruction Be?

Many teachers have implemented "academic checks" at various phases in the instructional process, and have thus utilized some of the instructional principles on which Precision Teaching is based. For example, the "trial test" on Wednesday and "final test" on Friday that has characterized many spelling curricula for decades represents one effort at focusing students on a curriculum-based assessment to facilitate learning during a single instructional unit. If students did not perform well on the Wednesday trial test, both the students and teachers could then determine which words required additional study, and that determination could be made before the end of the unit and the final test on Friday.

Using that as an example, we might reflect on the question, "How responsive to a student's lack of progress can teachers become?" Clearly, for many academic tasks, some type of daily assessment offers a very effective way to document if a student is benefiting from instruction or if additional instruction on particular content is necessary.

Finally, within the Precision Teaching literature, various guidelines are provided for calculation of appropriate rates of progress. For example, when a student's performance-monitoring chart doesn't indicate any progress over a three-day period, the teacher and student must collectively implement a modification in the instruction in order to initiate progress. Also, further guidelines are provided to calculate an appropriate rate of acceleration on academic performance. Thus, this intervention model offers practitioners one way to address the question: "How much academic growth is considered an appropriate response to intervention?" For that reason, we suggest that in-service training on RTI be based, in part, on Precision Teaching principles, and that PT be considered one basis for all RTI intervention models.

LD OR NOT LD? DOES STATUS CHANGE WITH IMPLEMENTATION OF RTI?

One additional concern regarding RTI implementation involves the question of who is likely to be identified as having a learning disability using RTI. Will the group of students identified using RTI be different from the group of students currently identified using the discrepancy practice? In particular, we believe that we can identify several groups of students whose status may change as a result of the implementation of RTI. This raises the question: Can a student have a learning disability one day and not have one the next, merely because the field chooses to change eligibility procedures while moving toward RTI as the major eligibility criteria?

What About Gifted Students With LD?

First, under current practice, some gifted students are identified as having a learning disability. Typically, such a gifted child would have an IQ in excess of 130 (i.e., two standard deviations above the norm on traditional assessments of IQ), whereas his or her achievement would be significantly below that (e.g., a standardized score on reading or math of 108 on a mathematically comparable scale). We might wish to ask, what is likely to happen to this child under RTI provisions?

Given that child's IQ and his or her reading performance, which is slightly above grade level, we would anticipate that the gifted LD child would fail to meet the criteria of Nonresponsiveness to Intervention under the new RTI provision. In short, this child is likely to respond to instruction to some degree, although he or she may not respond to instruction at a level commensurate with his or her IQ. Do we, as a field, intend to stop serving gifted students with learning disabilities altogether, and would that not be one predictable result of instituting RTI? As concerned professionals in the field, we have found no discussion of this question at all in the extant literature, but clearly it should be addressed as we move into RTI.

What About Nonverbal Learning Disabilities?

A second group of students that are currently identified as learning disabled who might be at risk for exclusion under RTI provisions is the group currently identified as nonverbal LD. Rourke and his colleagues (Rourke, 2005; Rourke, Ahmad, Collins, Hayman-Abello, Hayman-Abello, & Warriner, 2002) have suggested that various brain-imaging techniques have progressed to the point that learning disabilities may be identified by using these newly developed techniques (Rourke, van der Vlugt, & Rourke, 2002). Although historically an assumption has been made that learning disabilities are caused by some unspecified dysfunction in the brain, these researchers suggest that, using the modern brain-study technologies such as fMRIs, we can now document these brain dysfunctions (Rourke, 2005).

Specifically, Rourke and his colleagues (Rourke, 2005; Rourke, Ahmad, et al., 2002) have proposed two subtypes of learning disabilities, nonverbal learning disabilities and basic phonological processing disabilities. Given that almost all research on RTI has been implemented with students who have basic phonological processing difficulties, it is quite possible that the newly proposed RTI procedures would adequately identify those students. But what is to become of students with nonverbal learning disabilities?

Nonverbal learning disabilities are characterized by several factors including well-developed, single-word reading/spelling processing; efficient use of verbal information in social situations; onset of disability symptoms after the age of four years; excessive hyperactivity after four years of age; decreases in hyperactivity over the next decade of life; and possible withdrawal, anxiety, depression, and/or social-skill deficits in adolescence. This type of learning disability is notably different from the phonologically based learning disability. For example, the spelling errors of students with nonverbal learning disabilities are almost always phonetically accurate, whereas misspellings of students with phonologically based learning disabilities are frequently phonetically inaccurate (Rourke, 2005). Based on these initial findings concerning the differences between these two groups of children, both of whom manifest a learning disability using the discrepancy criteria, differential educational intervention options may be called for these two groups of kids. However, for our purposes here, questions must be asked. Specifically, it is quite possible that students with nonverbal LD could manifest significant achievement on various RTI interventions, yet still show a discrepancy between IQ and achievement, as well as display the characteristics previously listed. Do we intend to terminate services to this group of students with nonverbal LD if, as anticipated, their Tier One and Tier Two interventions show progress on various reading measures? Again, these students have a learning disability under the present guidelines, but may not demonstrate such a disability under RTI.

What About Students Who Are "Slow Learners"?

Finally, we have an additional concern about the students previously described as "slow learners." This group is not currently served under the "learning disabilities" category, because the group currently identified as learning disabled typically has an IQ of eighty-five or higher, and that exclusion criteria prohibits serving students with a lower IQ as learning disabled. However, does the RTI procedure open that door? Specifically, students with IQs between seventy and eighty-five—historically referred to as "slow learners"—have not been considered learning disabled because one criterion for LD was "normal intelligence." Therefore, these students have, in most school districts, not been eligible for services. If we terminate the use of IQ scores and consider how learners in this IQ/ability range may respond to the first two tiers of intervention under RTI, it is quite possible that these slower learners will not progress at an appropriate learning rate in those interventions. Are these students now to be considered as having a learning disability whereas before they had been excluded?

Alternatively, are we going to apply the same exclusion criteria and merely overlay the added requirement of RTI interventions? In most states, one had to demonstrate an IQ of eighty-five or above to be LD. However, the IQ eligibility criteria did vary somewhat; in some states, students with IQs over seventy were considered eligible for services as LD, and the state of California didn't use an IQ cutoff at all. Still, no guidance has been provided from the federal rules and regulations on continued use of this IQ cutoff; thus states are left to decide on their own as to continued use of this aspect of the LD criteria.

Of course, answers to these issues will significantly affect prevalence estimates for students with LD. As one example, consider the question: What will service of this group of students with IQs between seventy and eighty-five do to the prevalence estimates for LD?

As professionals in the field who deal with eligibility determinations frequently, we do feel that IQ assessments should continue to be administered for students suspected of having an LD, and that the traditional IQ cutoff of eighty-five should continue to be utilized in determination of the existence of LD. Although this recommendation is merely that—a recommendation—continued use of an IQ cutoff of eighty-five points or higher for students with learning disabilities would effectively prevent students with very low IQ scores from being identified as learning disabled. With that preference stated, the RTI process should certainly be employed for all students, including students with a lower IQ, because this does represent the best instructional practice available, and should result in high-quality instruction for those with a lower IQ.

When considered together, the aforementioned questions on how RTI may affect these various groups of students raise one scary possibility. It is possible that implementing RTI will result in highly selective provision of services, only for students with one type of learning disability (a phonologically based reading disability), while we begin to serve a large number of students with somewhat lower IQs, who have not previously been so identified. In short, do we intend, as a field, to "change out" the LD population entirely? At present, we cannot answer this question, but we do strongly feel that this question should be discussed by concerned professionals and parents, in the context of the implementation of RTI.

CONCLUSIONS

The overall question underlying this chapter is simple: "Will RTI deliver as promised?" Progress monitoring is effective as an instructional paradigm and the effort to mandate RTI as one strategy to deliver enhanced instructional efficacy for students with learning disabilities is applauded. In short, we support the implementation of RTI as an eligibility tool for documentation of and instruction for students with learning disabilities. We further believe that such implementation will have rather dramatic, positive benefits for all students, as teachers hone their skills in such a scientifically tested instructional procedure as RTI.

Still, there are unanswered questions and concerns about the implementation of RTI. To our knowledge, many of these issues have not been raised previously, let alone addressed in thoughtful debate. We need to consider, in professional debate, education of students who are both gifted and learning disabled, not to mention the nonverbal LD student. We need to consider the continued use of IQ as an eligibility cutoff criteria, and the many other issues raised in this chapter. Where possible, we have suggested procedures that we believe will increase the likelihood of successful implementation of RTI as an eligibility tool, and we have pointed out the advantages of RTI where we see positive benefit.

Most educators are motivated to serve students with learning disabilities in the most effective way possible. Of course, accuracy in identification is critical to that end. Still, these questions must be addressed by the thoughtful practitioner and researcher, with the best interest of the children we serve at heart. In moving into implementation of RTI, these questions should be addressed at the state, local, and school levels as a part of the training offered on RTI. On that basis, professionals, parents, and students with LD can come together and ensure that the most effective services possible are provided for LD students, as well as for all other students in our schools.

REFERENCES

Algozzine, R. (1985). Low achiever differentiation: Where's the beef? *Exceptional Children, 52,* 72–75.

Bradley, R., Danielson, L., & Doolittle, J. (2005). Response to intervention. *Journal of Learning Disabilities, 38*(6).

Coutinho, M. (1995). Who will be learning disabled after the reauthorization of IDEA? Two very distinct perspectives. *Journal of Learning Disabilities, 28,* 664–668.

Deno, S. L. (2003). Development in curriculum-based measurement. *Journal of Special Education, 37*(3), 184–192.

Deno, S., Grimes, J., Reschly, D., & Schrag, J. (2001). *Minneapolis Public Schools—Problem solving model: Review team report.* Unpublished paper.

Education of All Handicapped Children Act of 1975, Pub. L. 94–142 (5.6).

Finlan, T. G. (1992). Do state methods of quantifying a severe discrepancy result in fewer students with learning disabilities? *Learning Disability Quarterly, 15,* 129–135.

Fletcher, J. M., & Foorman, B. R. (1994). Issues in definition and measurement of learning disabilities: The need for early intervention. In G. R. Lyon (Ed.), *Frames of reference for the assessment of learning disabilities: New views on measurement issues* (pp. 185–200). Baltimore: Brooks.

Fletcher, J. M., Francis, D. J., Rourke, B. P., & Shaywitz, S. E. (1992). The validity of discrepancy-based definitions of reading disabilities. *Journal of Learning Disabilities, 25,* 555–561, 573.

Flugum, K. R., & Reschly, D. J. (1994). Prereferral interventions: Quality indices and outcomes. *Journal of School Psychology, 32*(1), 1–14.

Fuchs, D., & Fuchs, L. S. (2005). Responsiveness-to-intervention: A blueprint for practitioners, policymakers, and parents. *Teaching Exceptional Children, 38*(1), 57–61.

Fuchs, D., & Fuchs, L. S. (2006). Introduction to Response to intervention: What, why, and how valid is it? *Reading Research Quarterly, 41*(1), 93–98.

Fuchs, D., Fuchs, L. S., & Compton, D. L. (2004). Identifying reading disabilities by responsiveness-to-instruction: Specifying measures and criteria. *Learning Disability Quarterly, 27,* 216–227.

Gersten, R., & Dimino, J. A. (2006). RTI (Response to Intervention): Rethinking special education for students with reading difficulties (yet again). *Reading Research Quarterly, 41*(1), 99–108

Kavale, K. A., & Forness, S. R. (2000). What definitions of learning disability say and don't say: A critical analysis. *Journal of Learning Disabilities, 33,* 239–256.

Kavale, K. A., Holdnack, J. A., & Mostert, M. P. (2006). Responsiveness to intervention and the identification of specific learning disability: A critique and alternative proposal. *Learning Disability Quarterly, 29*(2), 113–127.

Marston, D. (2005). Tiers of Intervention in Responsiveness to Intervention: Prevention outcomes and learning disabilities identification patterns. *Journal of Learning Disabilities, 38*(6), 539–544.

Marston, D., Muyskens, P., Lau M., & Canter, A. (2003). Problem solving model for decision-making with high-incidence disabilities: The Minneapolis experience. *Learning Disabilities Research & Practice, 18*(3), 187–200.

O'Connor, R. (2003, December). *Tiers of intervention in kindergarten through third grade.* Paper presented at the National Research Center on Learning Disabilities Responsiveness-to-Intervention Symposium, Kansas City, MO. (See the discussion of this paper in Marston et al. 2003.)

President's Commission on Excellence in Special Education. (2002). *A new era: Revitalizing special education for children and their families.* Retrieved July 26, 2006, from www.ed.gov/inits/commissionsboards/index.html

Reschly, D. J., Hosp, J. L., & Schmied, C. M. (2003, August 20). *And miles to go. . . : State SLD requirements and authoritative recommendations.* Retrieved July 20, 2006, from www.nrcld.org

Rourke, B. P. (2005). Neuropsychology of learning disabilities: Past and present. *Learning Disability Quarterly, 28*(2), 11–114.

Rourke, B. P., Ahmad, S. A., Collins, D. W., Hayman-Abello, B. A., Hayman-Abello, S. E., & Warriner, E. M. (2002). Child-clinical/pediatric neuropsychology: Some recent advances. *Annual Review of Psychology, 53,* 309–339.

Rourke, B. P., van der Vlugt, H., & Rourke, S. B. (2002). *Practice of child-clinical neuropsychology: An introduction.* Lisse, The Netherlands: Swets & Zeitlinger.

Scruggs, T. W., & Mastropieri, M. A. (2002). On babies and bathwater: Addressing the problems of identification of learning disabilities. *Learning Disability Quarterly, 25*(2), 155–168

Spear-Swerling, L. (1999). Can we get there from here: Learning disabilities and future education policy. In R. J. Sternberg & L. Spear-Swerling (Eds.), *Perspectives on learning disabilities: Biological, cognitive, contextual* (pp. 250–276). Boulder, CO: Westview Press.

U.S. Department of Education. (2000). Twenty-second annual report to Congress on the implementation of the Individuals with Disabilities Education Act. Washington, DC: Author.

Vaughn, S. (2003, December). *How many tiers are needed for response to intervention to achieve acceptable prevention outcomes.* Presented at the National Research Center on Learning Disabilities Responsiveness-to-Intervention Symposium, Kansas City, MO.

Wagner, R. K., & Garon, T. (1999). Learning disabilities in perspective. In R. J. Sternberg & L. Spear-Swerling (Eds.), *Perspectives on learning disabilities: Biological, cognitive, contextual* (pp. 83–105). Boulder, CO: Westview Press.

White, O. R. (1985). Precision teaching—precision learning. *Exceptional Children, 52,* 522–534.

Wong, B.Y.L. (1996). *The ABCs of learning disabilities*. New York, Academic Press.

Ysseldyke, J. E., Algozzine, B., Richey, L., & Graden, J. P. (1982). Declaring students eligible for learning disability services. Why bother with the data? *Learning Disability Quarterly, 5,* 37–44.

Ysseldyke, J. E., Algozzine, B., Shinn, M. R., & McGue, M. (1982). Similarities and differences between low achievers and students classified leaning disabled. *Journal of Special Education, 16,* 73–85.

Appendix A

RTI Needs Assessment

Response to Intervention Needs Assessment

	Current level of implementation: 1 = None 2 = Some or beginning stages 3 = Most or advanced stages 4 = All or completed	Priority Level 1 = No 2 = Medium 3 = High	Comments: What does that mean for your school? What resources are required to achieve this?
General Education Curriculum			
All teachers are effectively trained in the curriculum standards for the grade level and content area in which they teach.			
Curriculum standards are implemented as designed in each content area.			
Teachers have a thorough understanding and knowledge of the principles and strategies of differentiated instruction.			
Instruction is differentiated by content, process, product, and learning environment on a consistent and ongoing basis.			
Curriculum mapping is utilized to align the curriculum across grade levels and content areas.			
Progress Monitoring			
Curriculum-Based Assessment/Measurement is used frequently to assess student progress.			
Teachers are trained in the use of Curriculum-Based Assessment/Measurement to evaluate student learning.			
Teachers have Curriculum-Based Assessment/Measurement tools available to them in their content area and appropriate grade level.			
Teachers understand how to analyze, chart, and interpret data.			
Teachers utilize data from ongoing CBA/M to drive instructional decisions on a daily and/or weekly basis.			

Response to Intervention Needs Assessment

Research-Based Strategies		
Teachers have knowledge base of multiple research-based strategies to address a wide variety of learning and behavior problems.		
Teachers have resources available to train them in specific research-based strategies.		
Teachers are trained in multiple research-based strategies.		
Teachers implement research-based strategies in their classroom with integrity and fidelity.		
A process is in place to ensure research-based strategies are implemented with integrity and fidelity.		
Standard Protocol Interventions		
The school has in place standard protocol interventions designed to address common and/or frequent learning or behavior problems.		
Flexible scheduling for students and staff is utilized to enable student access to standard protocols.		
Job responsibilities have been restructured to enable student access to standard protocols.		
Standard protocols are designed to assertively and intensively address student needs.		
Teachers are knowledgeable about or have resources available to inform them about appropriate interventions.		

(Continued)

Response to Intervention Needs Assessment (Continued)

Administrative Factors				
The entire administration portrays to the staff, students, and parents the importance of the RTI process for increased student achievement.				
The school schedule is designed to provide for flexibility and restructuring of resources to meet student needs.				
Various strategies including walk-throughs, extended observations, teacher conferences, lesson plan evaluations, and others are used to monitor implementation of research-based strategies.				
A variety of resources are identified and provided to address deficit areas in curriculum, behavior management, and instructional strategies.				
Teachers are provided with time and incentives for collaboration, professional growth, and staff development.				
Inventive programs for teacher training (e.g., action research, strategy sharing, publishing) are utilized.				
Partnerships are formed with local organizations (e.g., colleges, retired teacher associations, senior groups) for programs that directly affect teacher training and student performance.				
School and class data are utilized to determine areas of need.				
Adequate and appropriate resources to address identified needs are provided to staff.				

Response to Intervention Needs Assessment

Knowledge of English Language Learners			
Staff members have a good understanding of language acquisition theory and the effects of LI on L2.			
An expert in the area of English language learners is included in Tier Two intervention decisions for all ELLs.			
An expert in ELLs is included in RTI for all ELLs.			
Cultural Responsiveness			
Staff members utilize parent interviews, questionnaires, student records, previous teachers, and all other available resources to learn about students and factors that may contribute to their learning and/or behavior problems.			
Staff members are trained in understanding African American culture.			
Staff members are trained in understanding poverty and its effect on school performance.			
Staff members utilize their understanding of cultural differences to form relationships with students and to guide instruction.			

Appendix B

Georgia Pyramid of Intervention

In Georgia, the prereferral interventions that have been enacted since 1995 are referred to as the Student Support Team interventions, or SST interventions. With the move into RTI, you will see from the pyramid (Figure B.1) that in Georgia, Tier One and Tier Two interventions are the responsibility of the general education class and/or the existing supports in the school such as Reading First programs, early intervention programs, and other programs that are offered to every child in school who is struggling with academic work. Tier Three of this pyramid is driven by the SST and involves another, increasingly intensive, educational intervention. Tier Four, however, is implemented after an eligibility decision has been made, based on the failure of the interventions in Tiers One, Two, and Three to alleviate the educational problem. This is, therefore, a fairly standard example of a four-tier RTI model.

Figure B.1 Georgia Student Achievement Pyramid of Intervention

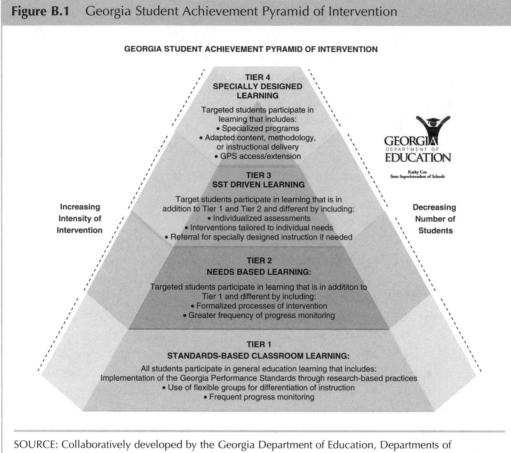

GEORGIA STUDENT ACHIEVEMENT PYRAMID OF INTERVENTION

TIER 4
SPECIALLY DESIGNED
LEARNING

Targeted students participate in
learning that includes:
• Specialized programs
• Adapted content, methodology,
or instructional delivery
• GPS access/extension

TIER 3
SST DRIVEN LEARNING

Target students participate in learning that is in
addition to Tier 1 and Tier 2 and different by including:
• Individualized assessments
• Interventions tailored to individual needs
• Referral for specially designed instruction if needed

TIER 2
NEEDS BASED LEARNING:

Targeted students participate in learning that is in addititon to
Tier 1 and different by including:
• Formalized processes of intervention
• Greater frequency of progress monitoring

TIER 1
STANDARDS-BASED CLASSROOM LEARNING:

All students participate in general education learning that includes:
Implementation of the Georgia Performance Standards through research-based practices
• Use of flexible groups for differentiation of instruction
• Frequent progress monitoring

Increasing
Intensity of
Intervention

Decreasing
Number of
Students

GEORGIA
DEPARTMENT OF
EDUCATION

Kathy Cox
State Superintendent of Schools

SOURCE: Collaboratively developed by the Georgia Department of Education, Departments of Curriculum and Instruction and Teacher and Student Support. Georgia Department of Education, Kathy Cox, State Superintendent of Schools, February 2006. All rights reserved.

Appendix C

*List of Scientifically Validated
Curricula and Other Resources*

There is no list of scientifically validated reading programs available from the federal government, nor is there even any consistency in what constitutes "scientific validation" for a curriculum. For example, does one research study in a peer-reviewed journal constitute scientific validation? If not, how many such studies are required to document that a curriculum is "scientifically validated"?

With those concerns noted, information is available on some of the most widely implemented reading curricula. This list is intended as a partial list of those curricula that have received some support and, thus, "scientific validation" from various scientific studies. This is not intended as a complete listing of all available reading curricula, nor is this an endorsement of the curricula listed below. For additional information, several Web sites are available that delineate the types of research support received by some of these curricula as well as other curricula. For additional information, the reader is referred to http://www.fcrr.org/FCRRReports or http://reading.uoregon.edu/curricula/or_rfc_review.php

Language! and *Language First!*	*Read 180*
Failure Free Reading	*REACH*
Accelerated Reader	*Read Naturally*
Classworks	*SIM—Strategic Instruction Model*
Corrective Reading	*Reading Rescue*
Great Leaps	*Smart Way Reading and Spelling*

REWARDS Plus	*Open Court (SRA)*
Breakthrough to Literacy	*Reading Mastery Plus (SRA)*
Saxon Phonics and Spelling	*Scott Foresman Reading*
Comprehension Plus	*Houghton Mifflin/Nation's Choice*
SRA Early Interventions in	*Reading 2003 (Macmillan/*
Reading Level I	*McGraw Hill)*
Destination Reading	*Rigby Literacy*
Wilson Reading System	*Wright Group Literacy*
Read XL	*Success for All*

Table C.1 Research-Based Strategies and Standard Protocol Interventions

Resource Name	Description
I've DIBEL'd, Now What? (Hall, 2006)	Instructional strategies correlated with each subtest of the DIBELS assessment
Differentiation Through Learning Styles and Memory (Sprenger, 2003)	Strategies for implementing DI based on learning styles
The Differentiated Classroom: Responding to the Needs of All Learners (Tomlinson, 1999)	Introduction to concepts of differentiated instruction
Differentiating Instruction in the Regular Classroom (Heacox, 2002)	Strategies for implementing DI
Fulfilling the Promise of the Differentiated Classroom: Strategies and Tools for Responsive Teaching (Tomlinson, 2003)	Strategies for implementing DI
Data Driven Differentiation in the Standards-Based Classroom (Gregory & Kuzmich, 2004)	Utilizing data to form instructional decisions in DI
What Successful Math Teachers Do, Grades 6–12 (Posmentier & Jaye, 2006)	Instructional Strategies for Math
Classroom Instruction That Works: Research-Based Strategies for Increasing Student Achievement (Marzano, Pickering, & Pollock, 2001)	Research-based learning strategies appropriate for all ages, especially upper grades. Not content specific—will generalize to all subjects
Catching Kids up (Thompson, Thomason, & Thompson, 2002)	Utilizing previewing strategies for concept development
How to Reach and Teach Children with ADD/ADHD (Rief, 2005)	Strategies and interventions for students with AD/HD
The Tough Kid Book: Practical Classroom Management Strategies (Rhode, Jenson, & Reavis, 1993)	Strategies for managing students with problem behaviors

Resource Name	Description
Error Patterns in Computation: Using Error Patterns to Improve Instruction (Ashlock, 1994)	Describes strategies for recognizing and analyzing errors in student work
Discipline in the Secondary Classroom: A Positive Approach to Behavior Management (Sprick, 2006)	Positive behavioral supports for middle and high schools
CHAMPS: A Proactive and Positive Approach to Classroom Management (Sprick, Garrison, & Howard, 1998)	Positive behavioral supports and classroom management for all grade levels
Whatever It Takes: How Professional Learning Communities Respond When Kids Don't Learn (DuFour et al., 2004)	School-wide standard protocol interventions
Relational Discipline: Strategies for in-Your Face Kids (Bender, 2002)	Positive behavioral supports
Differentiated Instructional Strategies: One Size Doesn't Fit All (Gregory & Chapman, 2007)	Differentiated instruction
Differentiating Instruction for Students With Learning Disabilities (Bender, 2002)	Differentiated instruction

Table C.2 Helpful Web Sites for Finding Interventions Appropriate for RTI

Web Site Address	Publication or Agency Name	Subject	Description of Contents
http://www.joewitt.org		Reading	Research-based intervention (Reading Center); STEEP RTI process and assessment
http://www.ed.gov/policy/elsec/guid/desi gningswpguid.doc	Designing Schoolwide Programs	All content	Developing schoolwide programs (word document)
http://www.cec.sped.org	Council for Exceptional Children		Legal updates, publications, and research
http://www.w-w-c.org	What Works Clearinghouse	All content	Evaluates programs and strategies in areas of elementary and middle school math, ELL, dropout prevention, character ed.; currently adding Reading and Early Childhood Education
http://curry.edschool.virginia.edu/reading /projects/garf	Georgia Reading First	Reading	Info on GA Reading First and numerous links
http://kc.vanderbilt.edu/pals	Peer-Assisted Learning Strategies	Reading and Math	Research-based strategy developed by Doug and Lynn Fuchs of Vanderbilt University
http://www.learningfocused.com	Learning Focused Schools	All content	Overview and information about LFS
http://www.ccboe.net/it/middle/lfs.html	Columbia County Schools	All content	Links to LFS and graphic organizers
http://www.everythingesl.net	Everything ESL	English language learners	Lesson plans, tips, differentiated instruction, ELL

Web Site Address	Publication or Agency Name	Subject	Description of Contents
http://www.lessonplanet.com		All content	Search engine for lesson plans, links, ELL
http://www.ldonline.org	Learning Disabilities online		LD resources
http://www.ldanatl.org	Learning Disabilities Association of America		LD resources, articles regarding research-based strategies
http://www.interventioncentral.org	Intervention Central	All content, CBM, behavior	Curriculum-based measurement, strategies
http://readingcomp.mathematica-mpr.com	National Study of the Effectiveness of Reading Comprehension Interventions	Reading	Evaluation of reading programs
http://www.osepideasthatwork.org/tool kit/index.asp	Office of Special Education Programs		Current information on research and resources
http://www.ncddr.org	National Center for the Dissemination of Disability Research		Research registry database
http://www.studentprogress.org	National Center on Student Progress Monitoring		Assessment
http://www.k8accesscenter.org	Access Center	All content	Research-based strategies, RTI information
http://coexgov.securesites.net	The Council for Excellence in Government		Program-assessment rating tool
http://www.whatworkshelpdesk.ed.gov	What Works Clearinghouse		Tools for assessing research-based practices

(Continued)

Table C.2 (Continued)

Web Site Address	Publication or Agency Name	Subject	Description of Contents
http://www.nichcy.org	National Dissemination Center for Children with Disabilities		Strategies
http://www.reading.org	International Reading Association	Reading	Reading research
http://www.nccrest.org	The National Center for Culturally Responsive Educational Systems		Strategies and info for ELL, African Americans
http://www.ncrel.org	Learning Point Associates™; North Central Regional Educational Laboratory®		Evidence of effectiveness for evaluating programs
http://www.rti.org	Research Triangle Institute		Research-based strategies including Making Schools Work (expanding High Schools That Work to middle schools)
http://www.gosbr.net	Scientifically-Based Research	Reading, Math, Writing, Assessment	Research-based strategies and assessment similar to DIBELS
http://people.cas.sc.edu/ardoins/pagesteep.htm	Home Page of Scott Ardoins, University of South Carolina		RTI process, STEEP, and CBM
http://bitwww1.psyc.lsu.edu/			RTI process, STEEP, and CBM
http://www.fcrr.org/Interventions/index.htm	Florida Center for Reading Research	Reading	Reading First, CBM
http://www.nap.edu/readingroom/books/prdyc/	Preventing Reading Difficulties in Young Children	Reading	Research-based reading strategies
http://www.nifl.gov	National Institute for Literacy	Reading	Reading strategies and links

Web Site Address	Publication or Agency Name	Subject	Description of Contents
http://www.sedl.org	Southwest Educational Development Laboratory		Research-based strategies
http://www.readingrockets.org	Reading rockets	Reading	Strategies for Reading
http://www.aft.org/pubs-reports/downloads/teachers/rocketsci.pdf	American Federation of Teachers	Reading	"Teaching is Rocket Science": Strategies for teaching Reading (PDF file)
http://www.ed.gov/programs/readingfirst/index.html	U.S. Department of Education	Reading	Reading First
http://www.learningfirst.org	Learning First Alliance	Reading, Math	Strategies
http://www.nationalreadingpanel.org/faq/faq.htm	National Reading Panel	Reading	Frequently Asked Questions
http://www.ncte.org	National Council for Teachers of English	Reading, English, ELL	Research and strategies
http://www.ahaprocess.com	Aha! Process, Inc.; Payne School Model	Cultural Diversity and Poverty	Strategies and research
http://reading.uoregon.edu	Big Ideas in Beginning Reading; Institute for the Development of Educational Achievement	Reading	Review of research-based programs
http://www.readwritethink.org		Reading and Writing	Lesson plans
http://www.thecenterweb.org	The Center Web		Links
http://www.ed.arizona.edu/celt/fs7.html	Center for Expansion of Language and Thinking	ELL	Strategies for bilingual learners
http://www.teach-nology.com			Strategies for content, ELL

(Continued)

Table C.2 (Continued)

Web Site Address	Publication or Agency Name	Subject	Description of Contents
http://coe.sdsu.edu/people/jmora/Mora Modules/default.htm		ELL	Modules for teaching ELL
http://www.metiri.com	Metiri (Technology) Group	Technology	Technology That Works in Schools (subscription required)
http://www.aimsweb.com	Aimsweb	Reading, Math, Spelling	Curriculum-based measurement tools, data-collection tools, and RTI package (subscription required)
http://www.isteep.com			RTI program including assessment, intervention database, and data management (subscription required)
www.renlearn.com	Accelerated Math™; Renaissance Place	Math	Instruction and data management (purchase required)
http://www.mhdigitallearning.com	McGraw Hill Digital Learning; Yearly Progress Pro		Data management (purchase required)
http://www.headsprout.com		Reading	Research-based reading intervention (purchase required)
http://www.cast.org			Research and products for Universal Design (materials available for purchase)

Appendix D

RTI Summary and Observation Forms

RTI SUMMARY FORM

Pupil _____ Date _____
Initiating Teacher's Name _____
School Address _____
Pupil's Grade _____ Pupil's Homeroom Teacher _____

Teacher's Statement of Academic Problem:

Description of Tier One Intervention:

Observation of General Instruction and Tier One Intervention:

Tier One Intervention Summary:

Post–Tier One Meeting Notes:

Observation of Instruction and Tier Two Intervention:

Tier Two Intervention Summary:

Copyright © 2007 by Corwin Press, Inc. All rights reserved. Reprinted from *Response to Intervention: A Practical Guide for Every Teacher*, by William N. Bender and Cara Shores. Thousand Oaks, CA: Corwin Press, www.corwinpress.com. Reproduction authorized only for the local school site or nonprofit organization that has purchased this book.

RTI OBSERVATION FORM

Student's Name _____ Date _____ Time of Observation _____

Teacher's Name _____ Observer's Name _____

School & Classroom _____

Effectiveness of Instruction: Note the Curriculum Utilized _____

Is this a scientifically validated curriculum? _____

_____

_____

Is an Instructor's Manual with lesson plans provided? _____

Did the teacher follow that plan? _____

Observation of Student's Learning:

Did the student demonstrate any particular learning style that you noted?

_____

_____

_____

_____

How did the student respond to the lesson? _____

Did you note any learning problems or student frustrations? _____

_____

_____

Copyright © 2007 by Corwin Press, Inc. All rights reserved. Reprinted from *Response to Intervention: A Practical Guide for Every Teacher*, by William N. Bender and Cara Shores. Thousand Oaks, CA: Corwin Press, www.corwinpress.com. Reproduction authorized only for the local school site or nonprofit organization that has purchased this book.

Appendix E

Where Do General Educators Find the Time to Do RTI?

William N. Bender and Cara Shores

Teachers will be challenged by RTI, and many will feel uncomfortable with the time requirements. Here is how we respond when teachers ask, "How do I find the time?"

RTI is one way to increase learning for all students, which is proven by research. This is best practice in 2006, and nothing less will do. Moreover, RTI is the morally right thing to do. When working hard to educate students with disabilities, the issue is one of civil rights and the national mandate to educate all children in the most effective way possible. These students also deserve an education; it simply takes more time for some kids than for others.

Next, negativity about time prohibitions have been wrong in the past. Personally, we've been around long enough to have heard this "can't make the time" argument many times, in various ways. Here are some other examples where a few teachers indicated they couldn't find the time. From the early 1970s, "We can't possibly do an IEP for every child with a disability." to the mid-1980s, "What do you mean do an intervention prior to referring a child for special education? What's this prereferral stuff about?" to the late 1990s, "We can't even manage the BD kids in the general education class, and now they want a BIP for all of them?" The answer is simple: our nation has made a decision; let's get on board and find out how to implement best teaching practices for the better education of the kids we all serve.

Now, after we've made that argument, we'll move on to possible solutions. Here are a few suggestions that might be possible in various school situations. We'll use the four-tier model from Georgia as the basis for this discussion. For the general education teacher in Georgia, we are talking about that teacher doing Tier One interventions, which is what he or she is already doing anyway—no time lost there. Next, that teacher will also be responsible for Tier Two interventions. In Tier Two, the implementation ideas that take relatively little time include:

- Do Tier Two interventions in the context of an ongoing intensive reading/math program such as early intervention programs, Title One, Reading First, etc.
- Train para-professionals to implement Tier Two interventions on a short-term basis. Para-professionals will, no doubt, be used for much of this, under the direction of a qualified teacher who reviews the performance monitoring.
- Use daily performance monitoring because it is most efficient. Using daily performance monitoring over four weeks yields more performance data than weekly performance monitoring over fifteen weeks.
- Implement Tier Two interventions as small-group interventions, as opposed to individual interventions. Para-professionals can work with three to five students at a time for Tier Two interventions.
- Schedule so a general education teacher has one hour per day to work with three different reading groups on intensive Tier Two interventions. You'd have to free the teacher's schedule by scheduling an activity for his or her class at a specific time each day, but that could accommodate small-group intensive instruction for up to fifteen students (i.e., fifteen students per group, twenty minutes per group, three groups per hour).
- Keep the daily progress monitoring in Tier Two simple and direct. Having a child do a reading fluency selection for two minutes gives a good measure of fluency; DIBELS on a weekly basis takes only a couple of minutes to give.

In all likelihood, various school districts will develop different ways to find the time for RTI. With that stated, the possible solutions here can provide educators with a place to start. Teachers should identify possible resources already available in their district, and be willing to reconfigure the jobs of various people for this RTI emphasis. However, the research efficacy of RTI suggests that such efforts will be worthwhile in terms of students' increased learning and improving test scores.

We are all going to be challenged by implementing RTI. Still, we are confident that caring professionals across the nation, working together for the best education possible for our students can accomplish miracles—they/we do it every day in the public schools of our nation. RTI represents the next step in education improvement and it is a step to take today.

Appendix F

Using Response to Intervention for
Inappropriate Behavior

We have stated several times in this text that RTI will dramatically change the way teachers teach. This is true because when this best-practice procedure is broadly employed, it is likely to increase teaching efficacy. RTI promises to increase student achievement, as teachers become more fluent in these practices. Thus, RTI may be envisioned as one way to address the issue of meeting adequate yearly progress toward school curricular standards.

The recent interest in RTI has been sparked because RTI is now recommended as the procedure to identify a learning disability. However, RTI is much more broad than merely an eligibility procedure. Many states are gearing up to implement RTI in a broader context that includes response to academic and/or behavioral interventions. Clearly, for documentation of a learning disability, an RTI procedure that employs academically oriented interventions would be appropriate. However, for curbing problem behaviors in the general education classroom, teachers should certainly feel free to implement an RTI procedure oriented toward behavioral change interventions.

Ohio, as one example, has determined that teachers in that state will move in the direction of implementing RTI for both academic and behavioral problems. The resulting RTI implementation plan in Ohio is referred to as "Ohio Interventions Systems Model," or OISM. Again, both academic interventions and behavioral change interventions are implemented under this model, thus increasing the impact of RTI in that state.

With this RTI emphasis becoming more widely discussed, we wanted to provide at least one example of how an RTI behavioral intervention procedure might work. Although our major emphasis in this text is implementation of RTI for determination of eligibility, once teachers learn the RTI procedure, they can easily implement it to address a wide range of behavior problems as well.

Imagine a young student, Gregory, in Grade 3, who has been calling other students names and demonstrating other types of verbal aggression since the beginning of school. Within only the first two weeks, the teacher, Ms. Lovorn, had begun an "ABC log," which notes each behavioral infraction in the class. That log noted some seven instances of verbal aggression by Gregory. The ABC log notes "antecedents of behavior, behavior, and consequences of behavior" (hence the term ABC log), and involves simply writing down a couple of sentences after each instance of inappropriate behavior. A sample ABC log of Gregory's behavior is presented in Figure F.1.

Ms. Lovorn had also talked with Gregory about his aggressive behavior. Finally, on two occasions, Ms. Lovorn called Gregory's mother by telephone and on those occasions, she sent home two notes describing this behavior. At the end of two weeks, Ms. Lovorn referred the problem of verbal aggression to the principal's office. Clearly, a more intensive intervention was required to address this problem.

A TIER ONE BEHAVIORAL RTI

In applying the three-tier model, the responsibility for the first intervention would rest with the general education teacher, Ms. Lovorn. Because the principal had already become involved, the principal and Ms. Lovorn discuss a Tier One intervention that will be employed with this child. Although Ms. Lovorn routinely offers reinforcement in her class for appropriate behavior (i.e., she has a "treat bag" and reinforces kids for correct work/appropriate behavior by holding the bag out for individual students to select a small treat—usually a piece of candy or small item such as a colored pencil, comb, etc.), the Tier One intervention these educators plan involves more substantive reinforcement. The principal and Ms. Lovorn jointly decide to implement a more intensive intervention by doing a behavioral contract for Gregory, stipulating additional reinforcement for appropriate behavior.

They wrote a brief behavioral intervention plan, which indicated that Ms. Lovorn would initially meet with Gregory to discuss his behavior. Gregory would learn that each day he was able to reduce his verbal aggression instances, he would receive ten minutes of computer time at the end of the day. He always enjoyed playing educational games on the

Figure F.1   An ABC Log

Name: *Gregory Hampstil*

Date: *8/16/06 – 8/25/06*

Antecedent	Behavior	Consequence
None observed: students walked into class at 7:50 AM on 8/16/06	G called out to Bobby, "I remember you! You're a son of a b ____!"	I spoke to G immediately and told him in front of everyone that we did not use inappropriate language or call others' names in my class.
8/16/06 1:45 PM Class discussion A student answered a question incorrectly, and G got excited while seated at his desk.	G said loudly, "You're an idiot!!"	The class giggled a bit, and I told them to be quiet, and then took G into the hallway. I talked to him again about his language, and told him not to do that or I'd have to speak to his Mom.
8/18/06 2:45 PM After the final bell as students left the class to head for the bus G was not particularly angry or upset.	G said, "I want to get to my bus first so I don't have to sit beside (he named another student in our class). He stinks!!"	I held G in class until the others had left (I knew his bus was last and wouldn't leave for a few minutes). I talked with him about how others felt when he said things like that. I then warned the bus driver.
8/20/06 9:35 on Thursday We were just beginning Spelling	G said, "I hate spelling and teachers that make me do it. They're real a __ __ holes!!"	I took G to the office for cursing and name calling. I talked with him on the walk up there about how his statement might make me feel. I shared this log with the Principal.
8/22/06 7:50 AM Monday morning	G came into class angry and upset. He shouted at me, "You didn't need to call my Mom! You turkey!"	I took him back to the Principal, and told him on the way that the Principal must have called his Mom. The Principal asked me to call her and request that she come to school for a meeting.
8/24/06 10:45 AM A student walked by G's desk and accidentally bumped G while G was writing a math problem.	G said, "You're an a __ hole and you better leave me alone."	Students giggled a bit and G looked surprised at that. I "fined" him some free time, since his Mom was coming in that afternoon to discuss these problems.
8/25/06 8:10 AM Just after class began	G said, "I don't want to be here. You're all a __ holes (his favorite term apparently), and you all hate me."	One student told him to "shut up," before I could intervene. I took G to the office. Note that his Mom did not show up for the requested appointment on these behavior problems.

137

computer; Ms. Lovorn felt this would be a great reinforcement for him. The plan also involved Ms. Lovorn continuing to maintain the ABC log, and thus "counting" Gregory's verbal aggression.

Unfortunately, after two weeks the ABC log included six additional instances of verbal aggression by Gregory. Thus, the Tier One intervention, although more intensive was not successful for Gregory. However, Ms. Lovorn did note one interesting fact during this intervention period. By implementing the more intensive intervention, she was able to note a bit more about Gregory's behavior. Ms. Lovorn noticed that when Gregory committed verbal aggression by calling other students names, he often did it almost without thinking. In short, she became convinced that Gregory was almost unaware of both his aggression and the impact of that aggression. This insight provided the basis for the Tier Two intervention.

A TIER TWO INTERVENTION

After Ms. Lovorn and the principal determined that the Tier One intervention was not successful, they met again with the special education teacher at the school. That team decided to embark on a more intensive intervention. Because Ms. Lovorn felt Gregory was "almost completely unaware" of his behavior, she and the special education teacher decided to implement a self-monitoring intervention. In self-monitoring, Gregory would be required to count his own verbal aggression, while Ms. Lovorn continued to monitor those behaviors using the ABC log. For an intervention using self-monitoring for decreasing inappropriate behavior, some degree of individual instruction is required, during which the teacher discusses, describes, and models inappropriate behavior and appropriate behavior, as well as the self-monitoring procedure itself. Then, a self-monitoring sheet is provided to Gregory each morning, and he is charged to "count" his behavior of calling others inappropriate names and other instances of verbal aggression. At the end of each day, if Gregory's count of his own behavior matches the count of Ms. Lovorn, Gregory earns fifteen minutes of computer time.

The team discussed the possibility of having the special education teacher consult daily in Ms. Lovorn's general education class while Gregory was implementing self-monitoring. The special education teacher did provide guidelines for Ms. Lovorn in terms of how to teach Gregory to self-monitor his own behavior. Once Ms. Lovorn had taught Gregory this relatively simple procedure, she didn't feel any further need for additional daily support from the special education teacher. Thus, in this instance, Ms. Lovorn implemented both the Tier One and Tier Two interventions relatively independently.

Figure F.2   Chart of Gregory's Verbal Aggression

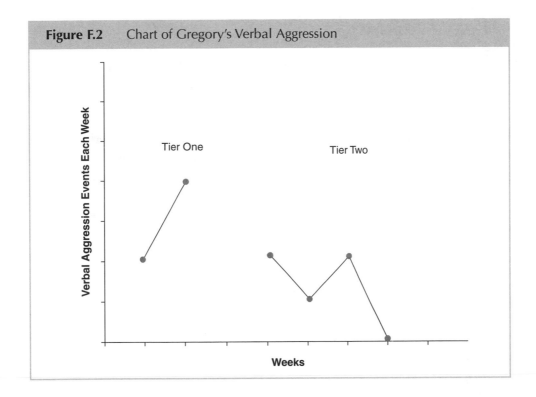

Ms. Lovorn charted Gregory's verbal aggression during the Tier One and Tier Two interventions; those data are presented in Figure F.2. As shown by those data, the intervention in Tier Two was effective over a four-week period in curbing Gregory's verbal aggressive behavior. Thus, in this instance, the Response to Intervention procedure helped eliminate an undesirable behavior.

A THIRD TIER INTERVENTION

In this example, a third-tier intervention is not necessary because the Tier Two intervention alleviated the behavior problem. However, in other cases where the first two interventions are not effective, it may be necessary to consider implementing a third-tier intervention. In applying the three-tier model proposed herein, the school-based eligibility team would conduct an eligibility meeting to consider the data from the first two interventions, and then determine if the child in question demonstrates a conduct disorder and/or emotional disturbance. Although no current state definitions of either conduct disorders or emotional disturbance emphasize RTI procedures as an eligibility tool specifically, eligibility teams would certainly want to consider data on previous interventions that were intended to curb misbehavior.

COMMON ELEMENTS IN RTI PROCEDURES

As exemplified in the previous example, implementation of RTI for behavioral problems has much in common with RTI oriented toward academic enhancement. The three-tier model is employed in both, as is the concept of increasingly intensive interventions in the various tiers. By increasing the intensity of intervention in each succeeding tier, many educational problems can and will be addressed in the context of the general education classroom. Further, like RTI for academic interventions, another assumption that underlies behaviorally oriented RTIs is the assumption that fewer students will require Tier Two or Tier Three interventions. In short, interventions in Tier One and/or Tier Two should alleviate the behavior problems before a third-tier intervention becomes necessary. Finally, as this example demonstrates, the general education teacher will assume primary responsibility for the interventions in Tier One, and possibly in Tier Two.

CONCLUSION

To reiterate, RTI is a very effective, "best-practice" teaching procedure that can and will dramatically enhance teaching efficacy. Further, given the application of RTI in both academic and behavioral enhancement, this procedure promises to affect schools rather drastically over the next few years. Finally, given the potentially powerful impact of RTI, it is quite possible, if not likely, that this procedure will become a critical method schools may use to address the increasing demands of adequate yearly progress (AYP). As such, teachers across the nation need to become fluent in implementation of RTI for both academic and behavioral interventions.

Index

**CORWIN
PRESS**

The Corwin Press logo—a raven striding across an open book—represents the union of courage and learning. Corwin Press is committed to improving education for all learners by publishing books and other professional development resources for those serving the field of PreK–12 education. By providing practical, hands-on materials, Corwin Press continues to carry out the promise of its motto: **"Helping Educators Do Their Work Better."**